HISTORY & GUIDE

Down

HISTORY & GUIDE

Down

IAN MAXWELL

The
History
Press
Ireland

First published 2010

The History Press Ireland
119 Lower Baggot Street
Dublin 2
www.thehistorypress.ie

British Library Cataloguing in Publication Data.
A catalogue record for this book is available from the British Library.

ISBN 978 1 8458 8958 6

Typesetting and origination by The History Press
Printed in Great Britain
Manufacturing managed by Jellyfish Print Solutions Ltd

Contents

Acknowledgements

Grateful thanks to Dr Ken Abraham, Newry & Mourne Museum, and the staff of the Public Record Office of Northern Ireland for all their help in supplying photographs and other material.

A very special word of thanks to my wife Valerie, who enthusiastically travelled the length and breadth of County Down, taking most of the contemporary photographs in this book. Thank you also to Andrew Grieve for taking photographs of Holywood.

To my sons Scott and Callum, thanks for boosting the economy of every town we visited!

And finally, my grateful thanks to Maeve, Stephanie, and all the staff at The History Press Ireland for their encouragement.

Historical Introduction

County Down has more than 200 miles of coastline. To the north, it is bounded by County Antrim and to the west by County Armagh and a small portion of County Louth. Topographically, County Down consists of low undulating hills from which, it is said, the county derived its name, Dunum, signifying 'a hill or a hilly county'. In the south of the county are the Mourne Mountains, of which Slieve Donard is the highest, at 2,796 feet. Much of the county's long coastline has been open to invasion from the sea but penetration into the interior was prevented by the Mourne Mountains in the south, the Castlereagh hills in the north, and the Slieve Croob hills in the heart of the county. Indeed, the mountains and hills created such a considerable barrier to movement across the county that the early major lines of communication followed the periphery. In the north of the county, Bangor and Newtownards are the most important towns, while the southern suburbs of Belfast are in County Down. Newry, to the south of the county, is a major commercial centre, which guards the narrow point between the mountains, known as the Gap of the North.

In ancient times, Down formed part of the ancient kingdom of the Ulaid, a confederation of kingdoms with its capital at Emhain Macha (Navan Fort), but little is known of these early inhabitants. They built a Bronze Age settlement at Emain Macha and consisted of several distinct groupings including the Ui Echach Coba, in the area that became the diocese of Dromore, and Dal Fiatach in the diocese of Down. At one time, the kingdom of Ulaid stretched as far south as the Boyne, but from the fifth century, thanks to a series of military defeats, they were confined to the area east of the Bann.

The Lecale region of County Down, between Strangford and Dundrum, is closely associated with St Patrick. Very little is known about St Patrick although it seems likely that he was a native of late Roman Britain. Much of our knowledge about the saint is gathered from *The Book of Armagh* written in AD 807 by the

Above: Mourne Mountains sweeping down to the sea.

Left: The Mourne Wall, from *The Illustrated Dublin Journal*, 18 January 1862.

master-scribe Ferdomnach. It contains a complete 'New Testament' bound up with accounts of Patrick's life and his 'Confession' in which Patrick defended his mission against its detractors. His object, he declared, was to bring the Christian faith to the Irish who lived 'at the ends of the earth'. Patrick identifies himself as the son of a deacon and the grandson of a priest. He mentions his capture at the age of sixteen during a raid on his father's estate, his escape, and his decision to return to Ireland as a missionary. The chieftain at the time, Dichu, gave Patrick a barn (sabhall in Gaelic, pronounced Saul) for holding services. Patrick was to die at Saul after more than thirty years in Ireland, and according to *The Book of Armagh*, he was buried on the great hill at Downpatrick.

Viking raids took place from the end of the eighth century. At Bangor, the monastery was sacked and its colony of monks slaughtered. Viking fleets were stationed in Carlingford Lough and Lough Neagh from which they launched attacks into County Down. Over the centuries, they were transformed into farmers, merchants, and colonists, but their legacy remains in the name Strangford, which is a word of Scandinavian origin, and according to tradition was so called because of the strong tidal currents the Viking raiders encountered.

The Dal Fiatach, the most important of the groupings or tribes of Ulaid, came to dominate the County Down region from their capital at Downpatrick. They believed themselves to be different from other Irish tribes, claiming descent from the 'Cruithne' or Picts from eastern Scotland. By the time of the Norman invasion, Ulaid was ruled by those bearing the surname of MacDuinn Shleibne (anglicised to MacDonlevy). The Normans overthrew the over-kingdom of Ulaid and replaced it with the earldom of Ulster. This was the consequence of an audacious expedition in early February 1177, when John de Courcy, a knight from Somerset, set out from Dublin with twenty-two mailed horsemen and some 300 foot-soldiers. He brought with him Flemish crossbowmen and Welsh longbowmen, who would pour down a deadly rain of bolts and arrows long before the Irish could get within range to use their shortbows and hurl their lances. The expedition marched through the plain of Muirhevna, over the Moyry Pass, into Ulster and reached Lecale in fewer than four days.

In front of Down, the capital of the kingdom of Dal Fiatach, the attack was prepared. According to the Anglo-Norman chronicler Gerald of Wales, 'John's followers were few in number, but good brave men, the pick of the army.' A fierce battle was fought on the open ground that slopes up south to Downpatrick from the River Quoile. After an intense and, for a long time, indecisive struggle between these unevenly matched forces, the Norman forces emerged victorious.

An even greater coalition of Irish chiefs joined for a final assault to oust the Normans in a great assault on Down in June 1177. The Normans triumphed again, and despite some serious military setbacks, de Courcy ruled his lands with all the independence of a medieval warlord. He minted his own halfpennies and farthings and administered law and order with the assistance of his seneschal, chamberlain, and constable. De Courcy also made generous grants to the Church including the Benedictine Black Abbey in the Ards. He encouraged devotion to St Patrick and was the patron of Jocelyn's *Life of St Patrick*.

Down, in Irish, *Dun da lethlas*, was renamed Downpatrick in honour of the patron saint and made an ecclesiastical centre. Grey Abbey, a Cistercian monastery, was founded by de Courcy's wife Affreca. The Latin name of this Cistercian Abbey is *Iugum Dei*, which means Yoke of God. The legend is that Affreca founded the Abbey in thanksgiving for a safe landing after a storm at sea. No Irish monks were admitted to the Norman monasteries. At Greyabbey, a colony was imported from Cumberland and at Inch Abbey monks were recruited from Furness Abbey in Lancashire.

The core of the Norman colony in Down lay in and around Strangford Lough; its security dependent on control of traffic on the lough. Although Carrickfergus became the chief port for both Antrim and Down, it was left to Strangford, Ardglass, and Dundrum to maintain trade and communications between many of the tower houses in Strangford Lough. Landing stages have been identified at Ringahaddy, Skettrick, and Mahee castles. Maintaining their dominance of the lough enabled the English to transport men and supplies quickly by water to and from trouble spots.

Left and opposite: Inch Abbey.

The Normans dominated the east coast of County Down for more than two centuries until they gradually became 'hibernicised'. Norman power was seriously undermined by Edward Bruce's invasion from Scotland in the early fourteenth century, and the decline was accelerated by the terrible effects of the Black Death after 1348. When the local Irish chiefs realised that the Dublin government was no longer able to move quickly to punish their misdemeanours, they became more unruly and audacious. The Magennises even occupied the royal castle at Dundrum. The fact that the Norman colony did not collapse completely was due to the tenacity of the Old English families, especially the Savage family and their followers – Russells, Fitzsymons, Audleys, Jordans, and Welshes – in holding the Lecale and the Little Ards (the name given to the southern part of that peninsula) while the White family continued to hold the barony of Dufferin. These names remain associated with this part of County Down to this day.

Meanwhile the Magennis clan emerged as the dominant Irish family in the western part of the county. The MacDonlevy family, rulers of Ulaid for centuries, apparently died out. The last recorded MacDonlevy 'king of the Irish of Ulster' supported William FitzWarin Seneschal of Ulster in 1273. The Magennis family ruled the kingdom or lordship of Ui Echach (anglicised to Iveagh) and were to remain in power from medieval times until the 1641 Rising. The family's principal stronghold was at Rathfriland, but by the sixteenth century there were four distinct families based at Rathfriland, Corgary, Kilwarlin, and Castlewellan.

The surname Magennis, with its variants Guinness, MacGuinness, MacNeice, and MacCreesh, comes from the Irish MacAonghusa, from the personal name Aonghus (Angus). The Magennises had a ceremony of induction for their chief, and their Coronation Stone was called *Coisleac Aonghuis* (the Footstone of Aongus). When a real Magennis was crowned it emitted 'a low pleasant humming sound', but if a usurper dared to put his foot on its sacred footmark, he was dashed to death on the ground. This Coronation Stone can still be found on the side of the old bridle road at Warrenpoint.

The English Crown never gave up its claim to the earldom of Ulster and encouraged the powerful Earls of Kildare to maintain the struggle by grants of land and authority in the Lecale after 1506. In 1515, the Earl was granted both the ports of Strangford and Ardglass with their tolls and customs. Even this project, however, had to be abandoned by the Crown after the Kildare rebellion of 1534, when Lord Offaly had proclaimed a Catholic crusade and besieged Dublin Castle. The Crown maintained an interest, by granting, to William Brabazon, in 1551, a lease to the manors of Lecale, Ardglass, and Strangford with all their ports, creeks, and islands.

There were always adventurers eager to take advantage of opportunities aris-ing from unrest in Ulster. The dissolution of the monasteries provided a certain Nicholas Bagenal from Straffordshire, in 1548, with a lease of lands that had been attached to the monastery at Newry. A few years later, he had the terms of his lease improved into a knight's fee, which made him the landlord. Although his property was devastated during the revolts of Shane O'Neill in the 1560s, his colony became quite a success, as confirmed in a rent-roll of 1575, which has survived. The surnames in the high street of his town of Newry produced an ethnic mix of English, Welsh, and Irish, while most of the names in the Irish of 'bayse' street were native. Many of these tenants had probably served on Bagenal's military campaigns.

By the end of Elizabeth's reign, England's piecemeal conquest of Ireland had now reached the borders of Ulster. Elizabeth maintained the policy of her father, Henry VIII, in trying to convert the Ulster chiefs into great lords on the English feudal pattern. She also attempted to establish a colony of English settlers in Down, under Sir Thomas Smith. He was given a grant in 1571 to establish settle-ments in the Ards peninsula. The colony failed, although Smith's family continued to advocate his legal claims for the next half-century.

Elizabeth pinned her hopes on the ablest of all the Ulster chiefs, Hugh O'Neill, Earl of Tyrone, who had ambitions to rule Ulster for the Crown. He had been brought up in England and, when war had broken out between the Crown and Shane O'Neill in 1566, had fought with the English forces. In 1585, he was for-merly recognised by the Crown as the Earl of Tyrone but he was proclaimed a traitor when he declared himself 'The O'Neill' ten years later. During the closing years of the reign of Queen Elizabeth I, a protracted and bloody war took place, with the native Irish forces scoring a succession of victories over the English armies. With the arrival of Lord Mountjoy as governor in 1600, the war began to turn in favour of the English Crown. Hugh O'Neill surrendered shortly after the accession of James I in 1603. He signed the Treaty of Mellifont in 1603 and was allowed to retain his lands in Ulster. However, his position was undermined by the presence of English officials and by garrisons, stationed throughout his lands. Therefore, in 1607, along with his family, retainers, and fellow lords, he fled to the continent.

Meanwhile in Down, James Hamilton and Hugh Montgomery exploited the particular difficulties of a local Irish chief, Con O'Neill, then imprisoned in Carrickfergus Castle. Montgomery engineered O'Neill's escape to Scotland and promised to intercede for him with the King, in return for a half-share of O'Neill's territory. At this stage James Hamilton wangled his way into the scheme. In 1605, the King ruled that Con O'Neill would retain an estate around Castlereagh, whereas Hamilton and Montgomery would divide the rest of north Down and the northern half of the Ards peninsula between them. Despite the intense rivalry between Hamilton and Montgomery, thousands of Scots poured into County Down and these colonies were to form the bridgehead through which Scots settlers spread out into Ulster for much of the seventeenth century.

When Hugh O'Neill and his supporters fled to the continent, the English Crown seized their lands, and in January 1608 a plan was published which called for the plantation of much of Ulster. Down, with its large settler population, was not part of the Plantation scheme. Although much of the county had been already been settled, the wars of the late sixteenth century had devastated the region. One traveller in Ards at the time of Queen Elizabeth described the area as, 'Scarce and starving – a country without happiness and without religion.' Sir James Hamilton established himself at Bangor, where he built 'a fayre stone house' using the 'rubbish' from the old monastery. By 1611, Bangor consisted of '80 newe houses, all inhabited with Scotyshmen and Englishmen'. Hamilton purchased from the Whytes, an Anglo-Irish family long settled in the area, the vast estates of Dufferin on the western shore of Strangford Lough, containing 1,600 cottages and nearly 30,000 acres. At Killyleagh, in this new demesne, he built himself 'a very strong castle, the lyk not in the North'.

Hamilton is said to have brought over 10,000 Scots to north-west Down. These Scots were mainly Presbyterian who were suffering under severe penalties, as Dissenters under the Anglican Church in Scotland. They arrived to find the country 'more wasted than America', and between Donaghadee and Newtown 'thirty cabins could not be found, nor any stone walls, but ruined, roofless churches, and a few vaults at Grey Abbey, and a stump of an old castle at Newtown'. Although County Down was not officially part of the plantation scheme during the seventeenth century, the fresh influx of settlers ensured that the native Irish were largely confined to the more remote parts of the county.

Meanwhile, Hugh Montgomery had built himself 'a princely mansion' at Newtown – later Newtownards – which, according to the Plantation Commissioners, had one hundred houses, all peopled with Scots. He constructed a jetty at Donaghadee and established a prosperous trade with Portpatrick and Stranraer. This was partially in response to complaints which had reached the king of smuggling 'at divers creekes of that coast and of bringnige in idle, leiwd and disloyall persons whoe decline the Justice of the kingdome where they lived and trouble the plantation in those partes'. Montgomery also persuaded a number

Belfast from Castlereagh.

of lairds from his own district to join him in Ulster and he gave them freehold estates of up to 1,000 acres; blacksmiths, carpenters and masons followed to construct the necessary buildings.

William Brereton, who travelled through Ireland as part of a grand tour which had taken him to Holland, the United Provinces, England and Scotland, left his impression of County Down during the mid-1630s:

> We left Dromore and went to the Newry, which is sixteen miles. This is a most difficult way for a stranger to find out. Herein we wandered, and being lost, fell amongst the Irish towns. The Irish houses are the poorest cabins I have seen, erected in the middle of fields and grounds, which they farm and rent. This is a wild country, not inhabited, planted nor enclosed, yet it would be good corn if it were husbanded. I gave an Irishman to bring us into the way a groat, who led us like a villain directly out of the way and so left us, so as by this deviation it was three hour before we came to Newry.

While the north of Down was taken over by the newcomers, much of the remainder of the county remained in the hands of the native families. After the defeat of Lord O'Neill, the Magennises had restored to them 22,000 acres in County Down, and Magennis of Iveagh was created a Viscount by James I. The Magennises retained much of their lands on the understanding that if they entered into rebellion against the Crown of England, the lands would be forfeited. Many of them found it difficult, however, to adapt to British concepts of money, landownership and mortgages. Sales of property took such a heavy toll on their wealth that by 1641 less than half of their patrimony was still in their hands. It was remarkable, however, that even those who lost their lands often continued to live on their estates as tenants.

Rebellion came on 23 September 1641. The insurrection is traditionally seen as a rising against the Ulster plantation but in fact the main conspirators were debt-ridden families who had benefited from the plantation. A series of harvest failures in 1629-33, combined with a general downturn in economic activity in the mid-1630s, left many Irish landlords in a poor financial condition. By the time of the rebellion, the Magennises of County Down were known to be heavily in debt. On the first day of the rebellion Sir Con Magennis captured Newry. He sent a message to the English commanders at Downpatrick and Dromore addressing them as 'my loving friends'. He explained his course of action in the following terms, 'We are for our lives and our liberties … We desire no blood to be shed but if you meane to shed our blood, be sure we will be ready as you for the purpose.' He demanded religious freedom and safeguards of their property rights and assured the authorities that the rising 'is no ways intended against our Sovereign Lord the King, nor the hurt of any of his subjects, eyther of the Inglish or Scottish nation, but onely for the defence and liberty of our selves and the Irish natives of this kingdom'.

The insurgents moved into south Down, burning the town of Downpatrick, overrunning estates, seizing cattle, and destroying crops. News of atrocities began to reach the authorities in London. In County Down, one of the best known was the murder of settlers at Lake Kernan, south-east of Gilford. In his deposition of 29 May 1645, Peter Hill, a former High Sheriff and Provost Marshal gives a graphic account of the massacre which took place at Lake Kernan in 1642. Peter Hill declared that:

> … about the beginning of March, 1641, about four score men, women and children of English and Scottish were sent by direction of Sir Phelim O'Neill from the county of Armagh down to Clandeboy in the County of Down, where they were met by one Capt. Phelim McArt McBrin and his company of Rebells (most of his own sept); which said Capt. McPhelim and his company carried and forced all these protestants from thence into a lough called Lough Kearnan in the same county in which Lough he and his said company forced them upon the ice and drowned them all, both men, women and children, sparing none of them at all.

Peter Hill had been informed by one Christopher Bellow that:

> … whereas Phelim McArt McBrinn and his wicked company had brought the four-score English and Scotts, that came out of the county of Armagh upon the said Lough, called Lough Kearne, and whereas they found it so frozen with ice that they could not

be drowned near the sides thereof; then they forced them as far as they could on the ice; but not daring to drive or pursue them for fear to break the ice under their own feet, and so to be drowned themselves; they, those wicked and merciless Irish, took the suckling children from their parents and them that carried them, and with all the strength they could threw them as far as they were able towards the place where the ice was weak and thin. Whereupon the parents, nurses and friends, striving to fetch off the children, went so far that they burst and broke through the ice; and then and there both they and then children perished together, save one man that escaped from them wounded, and a woman whose name we cannot expresse.

The settlers held a line from Dromore eastwards to the Ards Peninsula where they awaited reinforcements from Scotland. A large Irish force led by Sir Phelim O'Neill and Sir Conn Magennis attacked Lisnagarvey (Lisburn), where they were defeated and hundreds were slaughtered in the streets of the town. Major-General Robert Monro arrived at Carrickfergus on 3 April 1642 and moved southwards into County Down with his Scottish army. After a number of minor skirmishes, Monro encamped for the night in the woods of Kilwarlin. They reached Loughbrickland, where he put sixty Irish insurgents to the sword. Newry was reached later the same evening. Monro soon captured the town and a number of the rebel forces. According to Monro, 'the townmen were detained until trial should be made of their behaviour. We entered into examination of the townsmen if all were papists, and the indifferent being severed from the bad, whereof sixty and two priests, were shot and hanged, and the indifferent banished.'

Monro then moved inland, marching his undisciplined troops through Iveagh, Mourne and Kinelarty, leaving in their wake a trail of destruction and slaughter. By the summer of 1642, County Down was once again in the hands of the colonists and indictments for treason were issued against those, including fifty Magennises, who were accused of taking part in the rising. In the summer of 1649, Oliver Cromwell, having by then led the Parliamentary forces to victory over King Charles I, arrived in Ireland with an army, with the object of regaining control of the country and avenging the colonists who were massacred in 1641. This he did with characteristic ruthlessness. During the Cromwellian settlement that followed the suppression of the rising, 26 per cent of Down was seized and awarded to adventurers who had helped finance the war and the army who had put down the rebellion with such ferocity. Those lands belonging to Irish insurgents were confiscated and divided out under the supervision of a commission of the revenue established at Carrickfergus under the governor, Colonel Arthur Hill of Hillsborough. Forfeited lands at Rathfriland and Castlewellan were divided out among the adventurers, including William Hawkins who received over 21,000 acres. Thousands of Cromwellian soldiers were settled in the remaining forfeited lands in the county, principally those who had served with Lord Deputy Fleetwood and Captain John Barrett's troop of horse.

County Down, like much of Ulster, had been devastated by a decade of war. Nevertheless, for the remainder of the seventeenth century, increasing numbers of Scottish immigrants came to Ulster.

The settlers had to survive another great crisis when, in 1689, James II and William of Orange led continental armies to Ireland to fight for the English Crown. Panic among the settlers was increased by the contents of a letter found in the streets of Comber. The 'Comber Letter' was anonymous and it was addressed to the local Protestant landowner Lord Mount-Alexander. It warned 'that all our Irishmen through Ireland is sworn: that on the ninth day of this month they are all to fall on to kill and murder man, wife and child'. Copies of the letter were circulated among the settlers creating fears of another rising such as had happened in 1641. It was to have a profound effect on the citizens of Londonderry, where the gates of the city were shut against the Earl of Antrim and his Irish army.

In the middle of August 1689, the Williamite general the Duke of Schomberg landed his first 10,000 troops at Groomsport in County Down, before William himself arrived in Ulster the following June. The decisive battle was fought at the River Boyne on 12 July 1690 and this ensured the survival of the Ulster colonists. The Magennis family supported James II in the Williamite Wars and in the succeeding years many of their properties fell into the hands of settlers such as Arthur Hill, the soldier who founded the Downshire dynasty, William Hawkins, a London alderman who obtained an estate around Rathfriland, Francis Hall of Narrow Water, and Sir John Trevor.

Nevertheless, these new settlements did not attract sufficient colonists, and the majority of their tenants were Irish. They remained predominately Irish in character, especially in the barony of Upper Iveagh, where the Gaelic language still continued to be spoken until the early nineteenth century. These close-knit communities were sufficiently well organised under their traditional leaders to organise a parallel society to that of the newcomers, and those who wanted to work with them had to win their regard by treating them as equals.

After decades of unrest and bloodshed that had devastated much of the county, the eighteenth century ushered in a period of stability and, for many, prosperity thanks to the rapid expansion of the linen industry. Arthur Young, on a visit to Newtownards during the summer of 1776, noted that, 'If a weaver has, as most have, a crop of flax, the wife and daughter spin it and he weaves it; if he is not a weaver but employed by his farm, they carry the yarn to market.' Young found that further south in the barony of Lecale, 'The linen manufacture is carried on very generally throughout the barony. In Downpatrick, there are 500 webs sold every week.'

By the eighteenth century, local gentry, such as Lord Moira and the Earl of Hillsborough, promoted the development of the industry on their estates. Lord Moira hosted a dinner each Thursday for the cloth buyers who attended Ballynahinch market. By the close of the century, the finer branches of the trade, diaper and cambric, were boosted by the settlement of Huguenot exiles who settled in the vicinity of Lisburn, Lurgan, and Belfast. In the Waringstown area, the introduction of damask diapers is said to have been brought about by Samuel Waring who encouraged the settlement of a number of Flemish and Huguenot weavers in the area. Descendants of these colonists can be identified in local surnames such as Dupre, Pauley and Hillery and in name of the Dunkirk Road. A visitor to the village of Waringstown in 1740 commented:

> In this town and the neighbourhood of it the linen manufacture is carried on to great advantage, where it was introduced and cherished by the late Samuel Waring, Esq., well known for the great services he has the country in this trade, which has spread considerably here since that time that a colony of fine diaper weavers was transplanted lately from thence to Dundalk.

The Quakers, too, were very active in developing the linen industry in County Down. They settled in Lisburn, Lurgan, Magheralin, Banbridge, and Moyallan, decades before the arrival of the Huguenots. A Scottish Quaker named Alexander Christy is credited with introducing the linen industry to the Moyallon area. Edward Wakefield left an enthusiastic account of the linen industry in County Down in 1812:

> The whole tract is embellished with plantations; whether owing to the wealth created by the linen manufacture, or the trade carried on at Belfast and Newry, everything exhibits evident signs of increased population and industry. The banks of the rivers Bann and Lagan are covered with bleach fields, and present that cheerful pleasing scenery which characterises a manufacturing country and excites in the mind an idea of improved civilisation.

Newry established itself as an important commercial centre during the eighteenth century, with the construction of the Newry canal, started in 1730. When it was completed eleven years later it linked the town with both Carlingford Lough and Lough Neagh. Newry became an important port that served much of mid-Ulster; for a time the town competed with Belfast as the commercial capital of the North. White linen halls were built in Newry and Belfast in 1783 as both towns competed for the support of the northern linen-drapers. Despite its central position for the linen merchants of south Ulster and its links with Liverpool and Chester through its port, Newry could not keep pace with Belfast. Nevertheless, when Mr and Mrs Hall visited Newry during the 1840s they were favourably impressed, 'The houses are well-built, the streets remarkably clean and the sub-urbs in all directions are of great beauty.'

The mountainous area to the east of Newry remained wild and inhospitable until well into the eighteenth century. Chief Baron of the Irish Exchequer Edward Willes travelled through the area while on circuit in Ireland around 1759.

> Though but twenty-three miles,' he wrote to the Earl of Warick', 'it is a hard day's journey being over the Alpes and Apennines of Ireland: they are called the mountains of Mourne and the mountains of Newry. Within these twenty years it was an absolute uncivilised country, and any one who ventured to go among them did it as his peril, it being almost the inaccessible retreat of Tories and Raparees and outlaws.
>
> But a good road being made through the country, and some gentlemen who had land there being determined to improve it, it is much civilised to what it was.

He found the poor cabins scattered along the hills, 'the most miserable huts I ever saw, built with sods and turf, no chimney, the door made of an hurdle, the smoke goes all out of the door, the cocks and hens, pigs, goats and if perchance they have a cow, inhabit the same dwelling'.

Towards the end of the eighteenth century, there is ample evidence to show that there was a breakdown in law and order in County Down. The troubles of the 1780s and 1790s were caused by the increasingly subdivided land among Catholic and Protestant tenants, and to the jealousy of Protestants over the increasing entry of Catholics into commercial linen manufacture, which had earlier been dominated by Protestants. Soon the faction fighting that was endemic in rural society assumed a sectarian character. In 1785, an organisation known as 'the Protestant Boys', began to make an appearance in the North. They were more commonly referred to as 'Peep-o-Day Boys' because it was at dawn that its members took to appearing at the houses of Catholics and terrorising their occupants into abandoning their small-holdings. Local Catholics formed their own organisation called 'the Defenders', and in many parts of Ulster their aims became more militant, as they were influenced by events in France brought about by the Revolution. In September 1795, the Defenders assembled at Loughgall at the crossroads known as 'The Diamond' to face the Peep-o-Day Boys in battle. Following their victory, local Protestants formed the Orange Order which spread to many parts of County Down.

Down was also closely associated with Antrim in the rebellion of 1798. This is hardly surprising given the strongly Presbyterian character of the United Irishmen movement in Ulster. Belfast was an important centre of the movement. In 1791, the society of United Irishmen was formed in Peggy Barclay's tavern off High Street. In January 1792, they launched the *Northern Star* to promote the radical cause, with Samuel Neilson, owner of Belfast's largest woollen drapery business, as editor. The new organisation spread rapidly to the neighbouring counties of Antrim and Down. Its main aims were parliamentary reform and the removal of English control over Irish affairs. However, a copy of a document drafted by the secretary of a committee of United Irishmen near Ballynahinch for 1795 which has survived, shows that their programme of reform was largely based on a number of agrarian grievances. This manifesto is strongly Presbyterian in outlook, attacking those privileges reserved for the Establishment. Their demands included:

1st: Tithes will be abolished and every man will pay his own clergy.

2nd: Hearth-money – that abominable badge of slavery and oppression to the poor – will cease.

3rd: We will not thereafter be taxed to pay pensioners and sinecure placement to vote against us. The consequence of this will be that tobacco for which we now pay 10d per lb. Will then be had for 4d – Aye for 4d. – and every other article of imported goods cheap in proportion.

4th: We shall have no excise laws: the merchant and shopkeeper will get leave to carry on his business quietly, without the intrusion of plundering revenue officers.

The rebellion, when it came, was short-lived. It had already collapsed in the south and west of Ireland, when the standard was raised in the north. In County Antrim, an army of some 3,000 and 4,000 men under Henry Joy McCracken was crushed, but in County Down the rebels succeeded in occupying Saintfield. They were soon dislodged, however, by government forces under the command of Major-General George Nugent. Having burned Saintfield to the ground Nugent's troops reached Ballynahinch on the following day and proceeded to bombard the town. On the morning of 13 June 1798 the rebels' ammunition ran out and Nugent's army overwhelmed them on Ednavady Hill. No mercy was shown and Nugent later claimed to have killed 300 in the fighting and a further 200 in the pursuit. With the town a smoking ruin and bodies lying unburied in the streets, the rising in County Down was over.

During the nineteenth century, County Down did not escape the massive social and economic changes that affected the rest of the county. The rapid mechanisation of the linen industry resulted in local weavers being employed by mill owners under the putting-out system. James and William Murland erected the first successful spinning mill in the vicinity of Castlewellan, and mills were soon after established in Newry and the surrounding area including Dromolane, Mullaglass, and Bessbrook. Banbridge, Dromore, and Newtownards also became important manufacturing centres and the Dunbar mill at Gilford transformed it from a sleepy hamlet into a flourishing village.

In spite of the great social changes of the nineteenth century, the Scottish character of the county was still evident to Mr and Mrs Hall, who toured Ireland in the early 1840s:

> The people of county Down are, as a whole, of Scotch origin. There are, of course, numerous exceptions, but so small a proportion do they bear to the whole that the lowland or Ayrshire dialect was commonly spoken all over the county until about the middle or towards the end of the last century. At this moment a sort of mongrel Scotch is spoken in and near Ballynahinch, Dromara, Saintfield, Comber, Killinchy, Holywood, Bangor, Newtownards, Donaghadee, Kirkcubbin and Portaferry. The nearness of this county to the Mull of Galloway has made the districts on the town sides scarcely distinguishable, and the stream of Scottish population can be traced most distinctly from Donaghadee and Bangor towards the interior. The costume is much the same [as in] the remainder of the country. The men wear blue tail coats with bright buttons, corduroy trousers or drab, a showy waistcoat with glass buttons on Sundays, market days. They wear a good hat but when working a very old one, round which there is generally a piece of cord. The young females dress well but absurdly. A boa is indispensable, frequently a muff, a small bonnet, shoes with sandals and either a white or very bright coloured gown. An umbrella appears to be a necessary appendage, both to males and females.

Only a few years after Mr and Mrs Hall's visit to County Down, the Great Famine would have a devastating impact on the local population, already suffering from the impact of a recession in the linen industry. In 1845, the potato crop had been badly affected by the blight. When in July and August 1846 it struck again the impact was devastating throughout the county. During the bitter

Far left: First Presbyterian church Saintfield.

Left: Roman Catholic church Saintfield.

winter of 1846-7, a great deal of work was done by various voluntary groups. Societies, committees and individuals raised funds for the establishment of soup kitchens, which for many months provided a large section of the population with their only means of subsistence. The Rector of Tullylish, Mr William Butler Yeats, grandfather of the poet, used the local press to appeal for funds. In a letter to the editor of *The Newry Telegraph,* published on 21 January 1847, he sought to chastise those members of the local gentry who had not as yet made a contribution to the Tullylish/Gilford Relief Fund:

> Gentlemen, I am not ashamed to beg from you. I could only be ashamed of a refusal, or of worse – a miserable pittance doled out so as at once to attest the justice of the claim, and the hard, unfeeling heart of the donor … Upwards of three thousand persons, by the high price of food, are rendered wholly unable to support themselves: we have a moral claim upon you, as proprietors of the soil, to assist us in relieving such destitution.

By January 1847, the government at last began to realise that a radical change of policy was needed. A temporary Act was passed in February 1847 in order to establish soup kitchens, which would help bridge the gap until the harvest of the following autumn. On 25 February 1847, the editor of *The Newry Telegraph* drew attention to the fact that the soup kitchen which had been established in Newry was encouraging the poor from the outlying regions to come into the town:

For weeks past, there have been observable in our streets numbers of mendicants with whose faces frequency of their appearance had not rendered the community familiar … they travel into the town in quest of food, not obtainable in their own localities. Squalid objects they generally are. Their appearance sufficiently attests that their plea of want is no deceptive subterfuge. In nine cases out of every ten, moreover, in reply to your questioning, you have from these evidently distressed supplicants for alms the statement, that they had patiently endured privations rather than beg, but that, disease having been superinduced by insufficiency of the necessaries of life, and innutritiousness of the food scantily partaken of, they had had no alternative but either to allow sufferers from 'the complaint' to perish of hunger or come into Newry and seek for bread, no relief being obtainable in their part of the country.

The population of the county, which had stood at 361,446 in 1841, had dropped by more than 11 per cent in the first census taken after the worse years of the Great Famine. It continued to fall until after the First World War, and by the 1970s had still not reached its pre-Famine numbers. During the Famine, many sought refuge in local towns, such as Newry or Newtownards. The population of Gilford, which largely owed its existence to the firm of Dunbar, McMaster & Co. who had established a great linen mill in the village, more than quadrupled between 1841 and 1851.

Many migrated to Belfast in search of work and better wages. During the second half of the nineteenth century, the population of Belfast rose from 90,000 to 350,000. This had a major impact on many of County Down's towns and villages. Towns such as Downpatrick and Rathfriland, which were remote from Belfast, stagnated or declined. Donaghadee and Portaferry suffered with the development of Belfast Port and Larne in County Antrim. On the other hand, towns such as Newtownards flourished because of their proximity to Belfast, while others such as Banbridge and Comber were able to prosper as linen-producing centres until the decline of the industry, during the twentieth century. Domestic spinning and weaving of linen, which formed such an important element of the rural economy in County Down, was under pressure from the 1820s, as the linen industry became increasingly mechanised.

The arrival of the railways had a major impact on the economy of the county. They increased the level of mobility for people and encouraged the development of tourism. The Ulster Railway connected Belfast with Dublin with a major station at Newry. From Newry, a branch line made its way to Warrenpoint and Rostrevor. At one time the Banbridge Railway separated from the Ulster Railway near Lisburn, and passed through Hillsborough, Dromore and Mullafernaghan stations before reaching Banbridge. The Belfast and County Down Railway travelled through the centre of the county, running past stations at Knock and Belmont, Dundonald, Comber, Ballygowen, Saintfield, Ballinahinch, Crossgar, and Downpatrick. Places like Knock and Dundonald were still rural when the line was built in 1850-51, but the railway encouraged the building of fine houses for the commuters who moved out of Belfast to the suburbs. From Downpatrick, the Newcastle Railway took passengers to the coast, passing by the stations of Tullymurry and Dundrum. At Comber, a branch line took passengers to Donaghadee stopping at the stations of Newtownards and Groomsport Road on the way. Meanwhile the Belfast, Holywood, and Bangor Railway conveyed passengers along the north coast.

After the First World War, County Down was excluded from the jurisdiction of the government established in Dublin. Under the terms of the Government of Ireland Act, 1920, Down together with Antrim, Armagh, Fermanagh, Tyrone, and Londonderry formed the separate state of Northern Ireland within the United Kingdom. During the twentieth century, the linen industry continued to decline thanks to the introduction of new artificial fibres, high tariffs in the United States and competition from abroad. A *Guide to Ulster*, produced after the Second World War, bears witness to the impact of the decline in one of the county's most important industries:

> Flax, once an important Co. Down crop, now takes a less important place; the lovely bright green waving fields starred with blue flowers are no longer a familiar sight that they were once, and the Belfast mills now derive their main supplies from abroad. The rectangular flax-holes scattered everywhere along the streamlets and the frequent ruined small scutch-mills bear eloquent testimony to the decay of what was formerly a leading occupation.

In recent years, Down has been affected by the Troubles and the county has had its share of world headlines. However, the cessation of violence and the rejuvenation of the scenery, especially along the border, has brought new prosperity to the county. These days the growing number of museums and heritage centres, and the ageless beauty of the Mourne Mountains and Strangford Lough, continue to attract visitors from all over the world.

Chapter 1

Belfast to Bangor

Flying into the George Best International Airport along Belfast Lough, the visitor will get an early glimpse of County Down as represented by the Holywood Hills. Of the Holywood Hills, C.S. Lewis wrote:

> First of all, it is by Southern English standards bleak. The woods, for we have a few, are of small trees, rowan and birch and small fir. The fields are small, divided by ditches with ragged sea-nipped hedges on top of them. There is a good deal of gorse and many outcroppings of rock. Small abandoned quarries, filled with cold-looking water, are surprisingly numerous. There is nearly always a wind whistling through the grass. Where you see a man ploughing there will be gulls following him and pecking at the furrow. There are no field paths or rights of way, but that does not matter for everyone knows you – or if they do not know you, they know your kind and understand that you will shut gates and not walk over crops. Mushrooms are still felt to be common property, like the air. The soil has none of the rich chocolate or ocher you find in parts of England: it is pale – what Dyson calls 'the ancient, bitter earth'. But the grass is soft, rich, and sweet, and the cottages, always whitewashed and single storied and roofed with blue slate, light up the whole landscape.

Belfast is situated at the mouth of the River Lagan where it flows into Belfast Lough. The Lagan forms the boundary between counties Antrim and Down and although the sprawling city spreads into both counties, its heart remains in Antrim. Belfast is an industrial city, but no part of it is more than a few minutes walk from the surrounding countryside: most city centre streets offer a view of rolling hills or mountains. It is the County Down coastline, however, that has for centuries been the favoured destination of those escaping the city for the day. As Brendan Lehane pointed out in *The Companion Guide to Ireland*, published in 1973:

The south side of Belfast Lough is, naturally enough, the scene of Belfast citizens' relaxation and entertainment, especially at weekends. It is, as a result, a long stretch of resorts, with all the amenities resorts should have, but with many of the more interesting constructions of the past obscured by modern development.

So for those who fancy a little sea air, the A2 takes you from Belfast city centre to the popular seaside resort of Bangor. You will be following a trail originally made by Belfast's Victorian holiday makers and now largely the preserve of the modern-day commuter. Crossing the Queen's Bridge over the River Lagan, you enter historical County Down. The Sydenham Bypass takes you to the George Best International Airport through a part of Belfast that was once the preserve of its wealthier citizens. Of Sydenham, *McCombs Guide to Belfast*, 1861, observed:

> This is the name given to a highly-picturesque and healthy locality, on the slope gently ascending from the Downshire side of Belfast Lough, about a mile from the Eastern suburb … The advantages of the situation have already discovered themselves to the merchants of Belfast, several of whom have beautified the neighbourhood by the erection of splendid mansions, surrounded by ornate pleasure-grounds.

Twenty-five years later, Bassett described nearby Strandtown in his *Directory and Guide to County Down* as 'a beautiful suburb, occupied almost entirely by residences of business and professional men belonging to Belfast'. It had changed little by the time that the Lewis family moved to the area, when the author C.S. Lewis was seven. Little Lea, the Lewis family home from 1905 until 1930, still survives, although it remains a private residence. It was here that Lewis first took to writing as a hobby. Lewis's spiritual autobiography *Surprised by Joy* contains a few slender memories of his childhood home. The house, Lewis recalled, was:

> … almost a character in my story. I am a product of long corridors, empty sunlit rooms, upstair indoor silences, attics explored in solitude, distant noises of gurgling cisterns and pipes and the noise of the wind under the tiles. Also of endless books … From our front door we looked down over wide fields to Belfast Lough and across it to the long mountain line of the Antrim shore.

This area's association with Lewis is marked by the sculpture found at the Holywood Road Library. Here, Lewis is depicted as his fictional alter-ego Digory Kirke, from *The Magician's Nephew*, opening the door to the magic wardrobe. Although Lewis is buried in the churchyard of Holy Trinity church, Headington,

Oxford, County Down remained close to his heart. As he wrote in his autobiography, 'Heaven is Oxford lifted and placed in the middle of County Down.'

Four miles from Belfast, **Holywood** is beautifully situated on the eastern or County Down shore of Belfast Lough, and is backed by an extensive range of hills, which rise with a gentle slope from the water's edge. The town acquired its present name early in the twelfth-century Anglo-Norman invasion, when it was known by the Latin *sanctus boscus* meaning 'holy wood'. Before that it was known as *Ard Mhic Nasca*, meaning 'the height of MacNasca' and had been a place of some distinction since the seventh century, when a church is believed to have been founded in it by St Laisren. A short distance from the old church is a large ancient rath or funeral mound, a monument to some long-forgotten chief who dominated the area before St Laisren's time.

The area took on greater importance after the Anglo-Norman invasion, as can be seen in the defensive motte that was built by the Normans in the early thirteenth century, which can still be seen off Brook Street in the centre of Holywood, and by the fact that King John, when journeying from Carrickfergus to Downpatrick in July 1210, halted at Holywood. In about the year 1190, a **Franciscan priory** was founded near the ruins of the present old church, and occupied the site of the church founded by St Laisren. The priory was attached to the great monastic establishment at Bangor, founded by St Comgall, and with other monasteries at Newtownards and Movilla. It flourished for many centuries until it was dissolved on New Year's Day, 1541, by Henry VIII, with its lands passing into the hands of the O'Neill family and then to Sir James Hamilton, First Viscount of Clandeboye. The priory was attacked and destroyed by Sir Thomas Brian MacFelim O'Neill, Lord of Clannaboy, in 1572, in order to prevent Sir Thomas Smith, Secretary to Queen Elizabeth, from placing garrisons there. On 8 April 1644, a meeting of the Presbyterian clergy and laity was held at the priory, at which many of those in attendance joined with their co-religionists in Scotland and entered into 'a solemn league and covenant for the defence of the reformed religion, the safety of the king, and the peace, happiness, and security of the three kingdoms, and to secure and hold fast the league and covenant with England'.

The abbey ruins you see today in Holywood are those of the twelfth-century Anglo-Norman Augustinian establishment. The tower, however, dates from 1809 (the date marked on the original clock now in the current parish church) when this was the site of the town's parish church. In the graveyard which surrounds the old church, there are gravestones dating from 1630, and an elaborately carved stone of about six feet in height which was discovered some years ago embedded at a considerable depth on the north-east side of the old graveyard. It is now preserved in the belfry.

The present cruciform town plan, at the intersection of Church Road and Shore Road with High Street, derives from the Elizabethan Plantation of Sir James Hamilton, when Holywood was established as a market town. However, the settlement remained small (only thirty dwellings in 1800) until the early nineteenth century when it became a popular holiday resort for Belfast's wealthier citizens. According to Lewis's *Topographical Dictionary* of 1837:

> It contains at present 225 houses, mostly well built; bathing-lodges have been erected for the accommodation of visitors, a new road has been made along the shore, and a daily mail has been established. There are several good lodging-houses in the village and its environs; and from the increasing number of visitors, several houses in detached situations, and chiefly in the Elizabethan style of architecture, are now in progress of erection on the Cultra estate, by Thomas Ward, Esq., after designs by Millar. These houses are sheltered with thriving plantations, and beautifully situated on a gentle eminence commanding a richly diversified and extensive prospect of Carrickfergus bay, the Black mountain, Cave hill, the Carnmoney Mountains, and the town and castle of Carrickfergus, terminating with the basaltic columns of Black Head.

Above left: Lewis family at Little Lea.

Above right: Childhood home of Lewis.

Far left: C.S. Lewis statue, Belfast.

Left: C.S. Lewis.

Left: Holywood Maypole.

Below: Holywood Priory.

The railway line from Belfast to Holywood opened in 1848 and this led to rapid development of Holywood as a dormitory town. It was about this time that prosperous merchants constructed many of the substantial villas in spacious, wooded gardens on the higher ground along Victoria, Bangor and Church Roads. McComb, in his *Guide to Belfast*, published in 1861, thought Holywood a:

> … beautiful and rapidly-improving village and watering-place, situated four miles from Belfast, on the Downshire side of the lough, is well worthy of a visit from strangers. It may be regarded, in some respects, as the Kingstown of Belfast … One side of the entire road leading townward displays a succession of splendid mansions, groves, and pleasure-grounds. One of the principal buildings is 'The Palace' of the Lord Bishop of Down and Conor. In delightful situations, commanding extensive views of the bay and the picturesque shore on the Antrim side are numerous villas.

The building of the Holywood Bypass in the early 1970s has not diminished Holywood's popularity with visitors. Today it is a popular residential area and is well known for its fashionable shops, boutiques, arts and crafts. A **Maypole** (probably the last of its kind in Ireland) still stands at the junction of High Street, Shore Street and Church Street, which is an immense Canadian spar about eighty-five feet above ground and twenty feet under it. According to local folklore it dates from 1700, when a Dutch ship is said to have run aground on the shore nearby, and the crew erected the broken mast to show their appreciation of the assistance offered to them by the townsfolk. The maypole is still used for dancing at the annual May Day fair. The **First Presbyterian church** located on the Bangor Road opposite the Priory is also an impressive landmark, along with the **parish church of St Phillip and St James** in the Church Road area. All of these churches are listed for their special architectural and historic interest.

Just a few miles further along the A2 is the world-reknound **Ulster Folk and Transport Museum**, illustrating the social history and traditions of the people of Ulster. It comprises two separate museums, the Folk Museum and the Transport Museum. The **Folk Museum** houses a variety of old buildings and dwellings which have been collected from various parts of Ireland and rebuilt in the grounds of the museum. Visitors can stroll through a recreation of the period's countryside complete with farms, cottages, crops, livestock, and visit a typical Ulster town of the time called 'Ballycultra', featuring shops, churches, and both terraced and larger housing.

The **Transport Museum** houses an extensive transport collection, and tells the story of transport in Ireland from its early history to the modern era. It is the largest railway collection in Ireland. Steam locomotives, passenger carriages,

Above: Ulster Folk and Transport Museum.

Left: Titanic.

and goods wagons are combined with extensive railway memorabilia, interactive displays, and visitor facilities. The museum also boasts a permanent *Titanic* exhibition, documenting the construction, voyage, and eventual sinking of the ill-fated vessel. The ship has long been associated with Northern Ireland, as it was constructed in the Harland & Wolff shipyards, just a few miles from the museum.

A few miles further along the A2 is **Crawfordsburn**, a charmingly situated village, with an old-world inn, just two miles from Bangor. Crawfordsburn, named after a stream which flows through the village, originated in the seventeenth century as a small settlement on an important routeway along North Down. It has retained elements of its origins along its Main Street including the **Old Inn**, which has been in existence since the early seventeenth century. The mail coach running between Belfast and the port of Donaghadee changed horses at the inn, so it can claim many famous visitors including Swift, Tennyson, Thackeray, Dickens, and Trollope. It was also frequented by C.S. Lewis, who stayed at the inn during his honeymoon with his new wife Joy.

Nearby is **Crawfordsburn Country Park**, on the southern shores of Belfast Lough, which features a beautiful stretch of coastline and the two best beaches in the Belfast area. The park also includes Grey Point Fort, a coastal battery and gun emplacement, dating from 1904 and updated during the Second World War, which now houses a military museum.

Above left: Old Inn, Crawfordsburn.

Above right: Helen's Tower.

On the right of the main road near Bangor is the **Clandeboye** estate, seat of the Marquess of Dufferin and Ava, who traces his descent from Sir James Hamilton. Clandeboye was first settled in 1674, but the **Clandeboye House** of today dates from 1801. The house was enlarged in 1820 by Sir Richard Morrison, but the first Marquess, later Viceroy of India, altered the interior and the grounds in the 1850s. Clandeboye House is known for its series of intimate walled gardens adjoining the courtyard and house, including the Bee Garden and the Conservatory Garden. Further afield are the woodland gardens, which display a large collection of rhododendrons and other exotic species suited to the unique mild climate of this part of County Down.

The so-called **Helen's Tower** was built by the First Marquess of Dufferin and Ava, in 1861, in memory of his mother. There is one room on each of the three floors and a roof-bastion on which poems written by Tennyson, Browning and others are engraved. Browning's lines begin:

Who hears of Helen's Tower may dream perchance
How the Greek beauty from Scoean gate
Gazed on old friends unanimous in hate,
Death-doom'd because of her fair countenance.
Hearts would leap otherwise as they advance,
Lady to whom this tower is consecrate!
Like hers, the face once made all eyes elate,
Yet, unlike hers, was blessed by every glance …

From the top, there are superb views of Belfast Lough, the Irish Sea, and Scotland.

The Ulster Division trained under after the outbreak of the First World War. On 1 July 1916, the Division would take part in one of the bloodiest advances of the war during the Somme offensive. At 7.10a.m. on that fateful morning, the troops of the Ulster Division climbed out of their trenches and formed up in no-man's land. At 7.30a.m., the men advanced at a steady pace towards the German first line. Opposite Thiepval Wood the Ulster Division advanced as far as the German fourth line where whole companies were wiped out. West County man Wilfrid Spender was in a forward observation post and he left an historic account of the Thiepval offensive:

I saw them attack, beginning at a slow walk over no man's land, and then suddenly let loose as they charged over the two front lines of one enemy's trenches shouting 'no surrender boys'. The enemy's gun fire raked them from the left and the machine guns in a village enfiladed them of the right, but battalion after battalion came out of the awful wood as steadily as I have seen them at Ballykindler, Clandeboye or Shane's Castle. By night-fall all gains had been lost.

Spender wrote: 'I am not an Ulsterman, but yesterday, the 1 July, as I followed their amazing attack I felt that I would rather be an Ulsterman than anything else in the world.' The sacrifices made by the Ulster Division at the Somme are remembered by a replica of Helen's Tower, known as the Ulster Tower, constructed close to Thiepval Wood.

The four-mile tree-lined corridor of Clandeboye Avenue links the Clandeboye Estate to **Helen's Bay**. This avenue is a former coach lane built in 1850 by James Frazer for use by the Marquess of Clandeboye Estate to gain private access to the bay and later the railway station. The station, built in 1863, was the creation of Lord Dufferin, who constructed a private entrance and waiting room for his family. The planned village of Helen's Bay arose from the ambitions of the Marquess of Dufferin and Ava to develop the area as a luxury holiday resort to rival Portstewart and Portrush on the north Antrim coast. The granting of 'villa' or 'house-free' tickets by the Belfast and County Down Railway Company, which entitled the holders to free travel for a period of time if they constructed houses within one mile of the station, encouraged further development of the settlement. Visitors are attracted these days by its two lovely beaches flanking Crawfordsburn Country Park and one of the most beautiful golf courses in the north Down area.

The next town along the A2 is Bangor. It was the favoured holiday destination of Belfast citizens for generations, from its wealthiest merchants to its hard-pressed factory workers. According to Robin Bryans, writing in the mid-1960s when the homegrown seaside holiday was all most people could afford:

Ulster people do love to be beside the seaside and particularly at Bangor, which is a kind of Irish Southend. It is small, with most of the town near enough to the sea to fill its boarding houses. Behind the purple bloom of veronica hedges the bay windows look across the bay, themselves crammed with crowded high tea tables, where, in the centre of each one stands a kind of monstrance in this daily five o'clock ritual – the three-tier cake-stand.

Today Bangor, with a population of over 76,000 people, is County Down's largest town. In 2007, and again in 2008, the town was voted by Ulster Television viewers as the most desirable place to live in Northern Ireland, with excel-

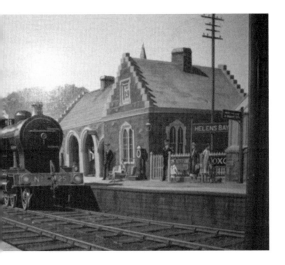 

Above left: Helen's Bay Railway Station in the 1950s.

Above right: Helen's Bay Railway Station today.

lent road and rail links to Belfast, which is only twelve miles away. Although Bangor seafront is mostly derelict, and waiting for the best part of the decade for redevelopment, the town retains the atmosphere of a traditional seaside resort. However, these days boating and yachting, sea angling, and golf are the main leisure activities.

Originally called 'Inver Beg' after the (now culverted) stream which ran past Bangor Abbey, the origins of the name Bangor are uncertain. The route of the name *beann* meaning 'point or peak' could refer to pointed rocks on the shore or to a pointed wattled enclosure as derived from the Irish word *Beannchor* meaning a horned or peaked curve, or perhaps a staked enclosure around the monastic settlement. According to *The Annals of Ulster* the monastery of Bangor was founded by St Comgall in approximately 555 and was where the *Antiphonarium Benchorense* was written, a copy of which can be seen in the town's heritage centre. The monastery had such widespread influence that the town is one of only four places in Ireland to be named in the *Hereford Mappa Mundi* in 1300.

The monastery situated at the head of the town, roughly where the Church of Ireland Bangor Abbey currently stands, became a centre of great learning and was among the most eminent of Europe's missionary institutions in the Early Middle Ages. However, it suffered greatly at the hands of Viking raiders in the eighth and ninth centuries. St Malachy was elected Abbot of the monastery in 1123. His extensive travels around Europe inspired him to rejuvenate the monasteries in Ireland, and he replaced the existing wooden huts with stone buildings. All that remains of these today is a solitary wall beside the current Bangor Abbey, supposed to be part of the monastery's refectory. Despite the decline of the monastery, its influence can still be observed in the modern town which boasts streets names such as Abbots Close and Abbots Walk.

The modern town had its origins in the early seventeenth century when James Hamilton, a Scot, arrived in Bangor, having been granted lands in north Down by King James I in 1605. Hamilton brought men from Ayrshire to build the town of Bangor, but its strongly Scottish character has been diluted as the town has grown. The Old Custom House, which was completed by Hamilton in 1637 after James I granted Bangor the status of a port in 1620, is a visible reminder of the new order introduced by Hamilton and his Scots settlers, and is one of the oldest buildings in Ireland to have been in continual use. You can get tourist information inside.

The town was an important source of customs revenue for the Crown and in the 1780s Colonel Robert Ward improved the harbour and promoted the cotton industries. Today's seafront was the location of several large steam-powered cotton mills, which employed over 300 people. The construction of a large stone Market House around this time, now used by the Northern Bank, was a testament to the increasing prosperity of the town.

The success of the cotton industry in the town led to rapid expansion for a time. By the middle of the nineteenth century, the cotton mills had declined and the town changed in character once again. Bangor soon became a fashionable resort for Victorian holidaymakers, as well as a desirable home to the wealthy. McComb, writing in the early 1860s, declared:

> Bangor, although not well adapted for a Winter residence, owing to the exposed nature of its situation, is a favourable Summer resort, being recommended by the purity of the sea-water and the atmosphere, its vicinity to Belfast, its numerous and comfortable lodgings, and its fine views of the Antrim coast.

Writing more than twenty years later Georg Bassett, in his Directory and Guide to County Down, was likewise impressed, 'There are few watering places where irregularity of the shore line produces a more pleasing diversity of scenic effects. The main street of the town descends a gentle hill to the bay, the formation of which is followed in the building of substantial houses.' The laying of the railway in 1865 meant that inexpensive travel from Belfast was possible, and working class people could afford for the first time to holiday in the town.

Old Custom House, Bangor.

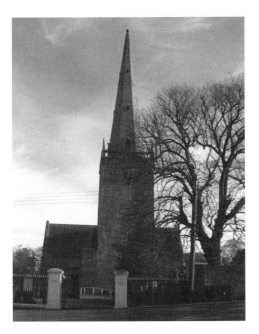

Bangor Abbey church and interior.

Queen Victoria visited the town and drove along the seafront, giving the road its current name of Queen's Parade. For generations of visitors, Bangor was Pickie Pool, an outdoor swimming arena, where many generations of Bangor and indeed Belfast children learned to swim. The bucket-and-spade holiday remained popular until the late 1970s when the package tour would take Ulster's holidaymakers to warmer climates. Up until then Bangor had, in the opinion of Robin Byrans:

> ... entirely escaped the crude vulgarities which have long been the affliction of every coastal resort in England. Bangor's skyline was still dominated by a slender church tower and a fringe of trees running across the hills behind. No great concrete hotels, brassy and blasé, crowded the seafront. It was possible to saunter along the simple promenade without being either gassed by carbon monoxide or maimed by impatient car drivers. Unlike Brighton or Bournemouth the streets had not been turned into car parks, and, if the mood so dictated, it was possible to get away out to the County Down countryside in a few minutes.

These days Bangor's once picturesque seafront is awaiting development, but the marina is the largest in Ireland. It is the setting for a variety of major sailing and tourist events each year. There is also much of historical interest to attract visitors. The impressive **Bangor Abbey parish church** has a fifteenth-century tower and octagonal spire dated 1693. When St Comgall's parish church was built in 1882, the Abbey was largely abandoned, though Lavens Ewart noted in 1886, 'The old church is carefully preserved and is used as a mortuary chapel, and for occasional children's services.'

Due to the increasing population, Bangor Abbey was brought back into use in 1917, and was reconstituted a parish church in 1941. Extensive renovations and alterations took place in 1960 and to a lesser extent again in 1995.

The main entrance into the church is through the West Door into the porch underneath the tower, the location of a number of interesting historic memorials. Just inside the doorway are two interesting Anglo-Norman stones, which were uncovered in the grounds of the Abbey graveyard. In the tower is the oldest tombstone in the church, that of Thomas Bradshaw, who died in 1620 and was buried in the ruins of the old church. Above the Bradshaw Stone now hangs 'The Rathgael Drum', which dates from the 1798 Rebellion. James Dowsett Rose-Cleland of Rathgael raised the Rathgael Yeoman Infantry, mainly composed of Orange yeomanry of the district, at his own expense in 1798. Rathgael yeomanry, under his command, fought at the battles of Saintfield and Ballynahinch. The drum has the names of these battles inscribed on it.

Above left: Bradshaw Stone, Bangor Abbey.
Above centre: Bangor Abbey Castle.
Above right: Bangor Customs House.

Bangor Marina.

Bangor Castle off Main Street was completed in 1852 for the Hon Robert Edward Ward. This imposing building is not so much a castle as an elegant mansion in the Elizabethan-Jacobean revival style. It has no fewer than thirty-five bedrooms and incorporates a huge salon for musical recitals. The stained-glass window at the southern end of the Music Room shows Edward III of England from whom the Ward family claimed descendancy. The Royal Arms are also shown, along with the Ward crest. The motto '*Sub Cruce Salus*' means 'Salvation under the Cross'. In 1973, the whole castle and lands were given to North Down Borough Council as a Council Building and the old music saloon is now used as the Council Chamber.

Today the **Castle Park** and its former lands accommodate two secondary schools, one primary school and the Institute of Higher Education, the Valentines playing fields, a Cineplex, council offices and a heritage site. There is also an arboretum and gardens for visitors to enjoy.

Bangor postcard *c.*1960.

Old castle, Bangor in the mid-nineteenth century.

Bangor Clock.

Another stretch of greenery in the town centre is **Ward Park**, once the site of the former brick works. Ward Park is renowned for its collection of wildfowl, some of them housed in breeding pens at the edge of the main pond. The formal gardens near the War Memorial are ablaze with colourful bedding plants and climbing roses in summer. There's no better place in Bangor to relax and unwind in tranquil surroundings and only a few minutes walk from the town centre.

The **McKee Clock** is situated at the foot of High Street is named after its benefactor William McKee, a local rates collector who donated £200 (a very large sum of money at the time) towards its construction. The clock was designed by Mr Bell, the town's surveyor, and built in 1915 by John McNeilly from stone quarried at Ballycullen, near Newtownards. On the base of the clock, a black granite slab is engraved with the inscription, '8 July 1915. This stone records the appreciation of the Bangor Urban District Council for the generous gift of this clock to his native town by James McKee. The above James McKee died on 28th April 1919.'

During the Second World War the Lutfwaffe dropped a bomb that landed on the top of the clock. Fortunately little damage resulted. Today the clock is a focal point in the town and a great place for native and visitor to meet and watch the world go by.

Chapter 2

The Ards Peninsula

The Ards Peninsula stretches twenty-three miles from Bangor to Ballyquintin Point at the southern tip of the peninsula. It varies in width from three to five miles and is a forty-mile circuit ending in Newtownards. This finger of land curving round the Down mainland contains some of the most charming villages and towns created by the Scottish and English settlers of the seventeenth century. In between these settlements are raths, holy wells, monastic ruins and old castles. This view of County Down was beautiful enough to tempt John Keats to cross from Scotland and to spend his one and only night on Irish soil at Donaghadee. Keats is said to have walked the thirty miles to Belfast and back from Donaghadee. He had intended to visit the Giant's Causeway, which he had been advised was forty-eight miles of walking. But, as he wrote, living in Ireland was 'thrice the expense of Scotland ... moreover we found those 48 miles to be Irish ones which reach to 70 English. So having walked to Belfast on one day and back to Donaghadee the next we left Ireland with a fair breeze.'

Bangor is an excellent starting point from which to explore the Ards Peninsula. Take the A2 to **Groomsport**, with its picturesque harbour. Groomsport's place in history was firmly fixed when, in 1689, William III's general Schomberg disembarked with 10,000 men to begin a journey which would end with his death at the Battle of the Boyne. By the late Victorian era Groomsport was chiefly known as a fishing village and coastguard station.

A few miles south from Groomsport is **Donaghadee**, which takes its name from the Irish *Domhnach Daoi* meaning 'Daoi's church'. The beach here consists of a fine stretch of sand varied by clusters of rocks, and although there are no high cliffs the coastline is a distinctly interesting one. A long pier stretches out to a lighthouse, which at night shows a red light that is visible to vessels twelve miles out at sea. The town has grown considerably in recent years with much residential development being a dormitory town of the greater Belfast area.

In former days Donaghadee was familiar to visitors from England, chiefly as the port of arrival on the shortest sea-crossing between Portpatrick in Scotland to the Irish coast. Construction of the current harbour began in 1821, initially under John Rennie and completed by his son, also called John Rennie. The **Motte** in Donaghadee was built to house the explosives for this blasting.

The establishment of the Stranraer–Larne service brought to an end Donaghee's role as a passenger crossing. Instead Donaghadee became a popular holiday resort. George Henry Bassett, writing in 1886, recorded:

> For many years the star of Donaghadee was in the ascendant, but it fell when the town ceased to be the landing place for the mails from Scotland … Donaghadee at present relies for success upon its manifold attractions as a sea-side summer resort. It has a splendid strand for bathing, and walks and drives, possessing numerous features of interest.

Robin Bryans, writing in the mid-1960s, showed that little had changed:

> Donaghadee was smaller than Bangor and more beautiful, it's moving bay the climax of the little bays of rocks and shale by the road from Bangor. None of the houses was more than three storeys and most were brightly painted, the Cafe de Luxe sharing the same facade of tiny Victorian houses with the Technical School. Donaghadee's bay extended to form a breakwater at one end, where fishing boats knocked each other on the rising and falling water. The Copeland Islands enclosed the bays other end almost making a lagoon of the gull-dotted waters. By a local tradition Peter the Great of Russia is said to have spent a night in Donaghadee when he came to watch boatbuilding in Belfast Lough.

The **parish church** is an ancient foundation, part of the tower running back to Norman times. The nave and transepts are Jacobean on Norman foundations. Originally they were in the Planters' Gothic style, though today most of the features, including the choir and the east window, are of nineteenth-century renovation. It is known for certain that a church existed on the site here at Donaghadee in 1622. Although it is highly likely that the site also had a medieval church going back several hundred years before, the date of the first church isn't known.

Evidence of the people's long association with the sea can be found in the tombstones of the merchants, fishermen and even deep-sea divers buried in the local churchyard. One such is that of Daniel Saul with its wonderfully nautical poem:

Above left: Donaghadee Lighthouse.

Above right: Donaghadee motte.

Beneath this stone lies Daniel Saul
Who round the world's terraqueous ball
Has sailed to every land was known
Now under hatches lies at home.
Anchor'd among his kindred mould
Dreads neither storms nor seas that roll
Brought to by death's correcting rod
Sets sail again to meet his God.

Grace Neill's, in the centre of Donaghadee, is, according to the *Guinness Book of Records*, Ireland's oldest public house, opened in 1611 as the 'King's Arms'. Situated on High Street, this popular little bar has many antiques displayed around its interior. Grace Neill was a patron of the pub, and a Donaghadee resident who lived for ninety-eight years until 1918. The pub was renamed in her honour and her benign ghost is said to be present in the building to this day.

South from Donaghadee along the A2 is **Millisle**, with its acres of caravan sites among the sand-dunes. Near Millisle is **Ballycopeland Windmill**, the last working mill in County Down which, at the beginning of the nineteenth century, boasted over one hundred examples. It was built in *c.*1790, and remained in use until 1915. Now in the hands of the Northern Ireland Environment Agency, it has been fully restored and is open to the public.

Far left: Donaghadee, *c.*1910.

Left: Donaghadee parish church.

Inland between Millisle and Ballywater is **Carrowdore** which is a small village with the unusual distinction of having the widest main street in the United Kingdom. Carrowdore was once renowned for the now-extinct Carrowdore 100 motorcycle Road Race which was started in 1927. Louis MacNeice, one of the country's greatest poets, is buried at the Church of Ireland church, in the village. He died on 4 September 1963 in London and is buried beside his mother (who died of TB when he was a child) and his grandfather. Fellow Ulster poet Derek Mahon wrote an elegy for MacNeice entitled 'In Carrowdore Churchyard'.

Follow the A2 south until you reach **Ballywalter**. In 1661, the village was described as having twenty-four tenements and by 1681 there was a water mill, a windmill, three tenements, a slate quarry and a creek for small boats to land. By 1744 it was described as a pretty little village with a slate quarry and a nearby Presbyterian church. The extent to which the people of Ballywalter were involved in the 1798 Rebellion is illustrated by an announcement in the *Freeman's Journal* on 11 August 1798. It stated that:

> ... the magnitude of the punishment of many districts of County Down may be conceived from this single fact – of the inhabitants of the little village of Ballywalter nine men were actually killed and thirteen returned wounded, victims of their folly. If a trifling village suffered so much what must have been the aggregate loss in those parts of the country which were in a state of rebellion.

Today, Ballywalter has a small population, which grows during the summer season with tourists and people with holiday homes who descend on the town for the beautiful coastal scenery. **Ballywalter Park** is a stately home on the outskirts of Ballywalter, which is open to the public by appointment, as the Mulholland family still live on the estate. The park plays host to the Northern Ireland Game Fair, which attracts nearly 40,000 people over a single weekend. **Templefinn,** alias **White church**, is a medieval parish church situated just to the north of the village. At the east gable of the church are three Anglo-Norman grave slabs.

South along the A2, **Ballyhalbert** is largely residential village with a small harbour and large caravan site which was formerly an RAF base. The name Ballyhalbert is derived from the Irish *Baile Thalbóid* meaning 'Talbóid's (Talbot's) town'. The Talbot family settled in the area following the Norman invasion of the twelfth century. There is an ancient Anglo-Norman motte just behind the village. By the early Victorian period its inhabitants were mostly fishermen. The village played a major role during the Second World War, protecting Belfast and the eastern half of Northern Ireland. **Burr Point** at Ballyhalbert is the most easterly place in Ireland, though some say **Burial Island**, the islet offshore occupied by seals, ought to count as being even more easterly.

Inland from Ballyhalbert is **Kirkiston** which is situated near the fishing village of Portavogie and has been home to the 500 Motor Racing Club of Ireland since 1953. Many of the fishermen who settled here were 'Covenanters' who had come from Scotland to escape persecution. **Kirkistown Castle** is a castle situated near Cloghy. It is an impressive three-storey tower house, built in 1622 by Roland Savage, at the site of a ninth-century round tower. It was occupied until 1731, when it was finally abandoned.

Back on the A2, south of Ballyhalbert is **Portavogie** (from the Irish: *Port an Bhogaigh* meaning 'harbour of the bog'). The town has a modern harbour, housing a large fishing fleet catching mainly prawns and herrings. This quiet fishing village is the second largest fishing port in County Down next to Kilkeel. Most evenings there are fish auctions on the quays.

South of Portavogie is **Cloghy** or Cloughey. The present village of Cloghy is a ribbon development following the main road which runs roughly parallel with the shoreline for almost the entire length of Cloghy Bay. Between the wars, Cloghy became a popular holiday location and many of the houses along Main Road and Quarter Road (close to the golf course and the beach) were built as holiday homes in this period. **The White House** is a ruined seventeenth-century dwelling house at Ballyspurge, near Cloghy. Sources suggest that it was built in about 1634 by Roland Savage. The gabled house had a steeply pitched roof and thick walls, pierced by pistol-loops for defence.

Portaferry, from *Port an Pheire* meaning 'landing place of the ferry', is a small but picturesque town at the southern end of the Ards Peninsula, near the Narrows at the entrance to Stangford Lough. It has an aquarium and is well known for the annual Galway Hookers Regatta. There are impressive Georgian buildings in the town square, including a fine Market House.

Above left:
Ballycopeland
Windmill.

Above right:
Carrowdore Castle.

Far left: Standing
Stone with motte in
the background.

Left: Kirkistown Castle.

Portaferry shows signs of its Norman association in castle stumps and old-fashioned streets of haphazard plan. The town owes its origin to a castle built by the first of the Savage family, who came into this part of the country with John de Courcy, shortly after the arrival of the Anglo-Normans. Its situation on the strait made it a post of great importance in all the subsequent wars, during which neither it nor the neighbouring district of the Southern Ardes ever fell into the hands of the native Irish. During the Rebellion of 1798 the yeomanry routed a rebel force in the Market Square of the town forcing them to retreat. The **Market House** occupied by the yeomanry survives and is now used as a community centre. According to Lewis' *Topographical Dictionary* of 1837:

... the town, until lately, was only a small collection of cottages, built under the shelter of the castle, and chiefly inhabited by fishermen. It is now, owing to the exertions of the proprietor, Andrew Nugent, Esq., and the spirit of commercial enterprise in the principal townsmen, a place of considerable business, and increasing yearly in prosperity. It consists of a square and three principal streets, besides a range of good houses on the quay, which is built along the edge of the strait, chiefly at the expense of Mr. Nugent.

Portaferry today.

In his 1886 guide, Bassett thought Portaferry 'deserves to be classed among the most charming picturesque places in Ireland'. Portaferry in the twenty-first century has retained its charm. One of things for which it is best known is the ferry between Portaferry and Strangford, which was established by Queen Anne who provided a royal grant for its maintenance. Robin Bryans wrote in the 1960s:

> It is an interesting experience to shoot out of the placid deep harbour, with water so clear that the bottom is distinctly visible thirty feet down, and immediately to be seized upon by black eddies, which tear you away from the shore with alarming rapidity. For five minutes you are swept towards the open sea, then a ridge of milk-white bubbles denotes a counter-tide. Your bow swings and you shoot as rapidly in the other direction. Within another five minutes the harbour of Strangford with its island bar closes around you, and the water is again placid, deep, and clear. It is hard to credit that the channel between these two towns is as deep as that between Dover and Calais.

These days, the Roads Service (Department for Regional Development) operates a car-ferry service across Strangford Lough between the villages of Strangford and Portaferry. To travel the distance between Strangford and Portaferry by road is approximately seventy-five kilometres and takes about an hour and a half by car. By contrast, the ferry route is approximately 0.6 nautical miles (1.1 km) with a typical crossing time of about eight minutes.

Overlooking the harbour is **Portaferry Castle**, a small sixteenth-century tower house built by William Savage. It is a square building, with a small projecting turret on the south corner. Most of the eastern corner is in ruins. The entrance at the base of the tower is protected by a small machicolation and the entrance to the ground-floor chamber is protected by a murder-hole. A curved stairway within the tower rises to the first floor and a spiral stairway in the west corner continues to roof level.

In Castle Street is the **Aquarium Exploris** where, in spacious tanks, you can see many of the sea animals that inhabit Strangford Lough. A visit to Exploris enables the visitor to view and learn about the marine species that are indigenous to Strangford Lough and the coastline of the island. The Open Sea Tank, the largest tank in the aquarium, contains animals of the open sea such as sharks, conger eels, and rays. Touchtank demonstrations, delivered by experienced guides, run at regular intervals throughout the day. These not only give visitors the chance to have their questions about our local marine life answered but also to touch and hold a number of species.

Turning north from Portaferrry on the A20 through Ardkeen is the village of **Kircubbin**, from the Irish *Cill Ghobáin* meaning 'Church of (St) Ghobán.' This possible translation of the Irish name is the only evidence that connects the Irish Saint Goban to the village. The village harbour contains leisure craft, yachts, and a sailing club. The main street is lined with old houses, many of which used to have stables behind them. Kircubbin (then known as *Cubinhillis*) and nearby Inishargy are mentioned in early medieval records. John de Courcy brought Benedictines from Stoke Courcy in Somerset and Lonlay in France, for whom he founded Black Abbey (St Andrews in Ards), near Inishargy in the 1180s.

A couple of miles down the road you reach **Greyabbey**, home to a Cistercian Abbey founded in 1193 by Affreca, daughter of the King of Man, who married John de Courcy. The village has retained its Georgian charm, and today is known for its antique shops, coaching inn, and tea rooms. The ruins of the Cistercian Abbey church and living quarters are one of the best examples of Anglo-Norman religious architecture in Northern Ireland. Tradition says that Affreca founded the abbey in thanksgiving for a safe landing after a perilous journey at sea. The abbey was colonised with monks from Holmcultram in Cumberland, with which it maintained close ties in the early years. Little is known of the abbey's history, though it appears to have been almost completely destroyed during the invasion of Edward Bruce (1315-18). The abbey was dissolved in 1541 and part of the monastic property was granted to Gerald, Earl of Kildare. In 1572, Brian O'Neill burnt Grey Abbey in order to stop it being used as a refuge for English colonists trying to settle in the Ards Peninsula. In the seventeenth century the church nave was re-roofed and served as a parish church until 1778. In the late nineteenth century repairs were executed by the Commissioner of Public Works. Unfortunately, an excessive amount of concrete was used, the crudity of which is still obvious today.

For those who enjoy stately homes there is much of interest in the area. Near the village is **Grey Abbey House** which has been in the possession of the Montgomery family since 1607, when Sir Hugh Montgomery (later 1st Viscount Montgomery of The Great Ards) arrived in County Down from lowland Scotland. Built in 1762, the present house is considered to be one of the finest Georgian country houses in Ireland. The house contains interesting architectural features and fine eighteenth-century plasterwork. James Boswell visited 'the excellent house of Mr. Montgomery's own planning' in 1769. Boswell commented on the fine views overlooking Strangford Lough. Visiting the house, today, is by appointment only.

Greyabbey village.

Above left: Greyabbey, from *The Illustrated London Journal*, 1862.

Above right: Mount Stewart Temple of the Winds.

A short distance away is **Mount Stewart**, the seat of the Stewart family (later Vane-Tempest-Stewart). They are better known as the holders of the title Marquess of Londonderry. The house and gardens remain one of the National Trust's most popular attractions. The house, a long, low and deceptively-large classical building overlooking Strangford Lough, has undergone many changes by successive generations of the family, most recently by Edith, wife of the seventh Marquess, during the interwar years. There is a guided tour of the house, which lets you see all the amazing paintings and luxuriously-decorated rooms, as well as the full history behind them.

The famous gardens at Mount Stewart were planted in the 1920s by Edith, Lady Londonderry, and are of international importance. The magnificent series of outdoor 'rooms' and vibrant parterres contain many rare plants that thrive in the mild climate of the Ards Peninsula. The **Temple of the Winds** is an octagonal building which was inspired by the Grand Tour the 1st Marquess took in his youth. **Tir Na Nog** is the Vane-Tempest-Stewart's burial ground. The 7th Marquess and his wife are buried here surrounded by statues of Irish saints.

Chapter 3

Belfast to mid-Down

The legendary travel writer H.V. Morton travelled into County Down from Belfast in 1930 and found it, 'a place of little friendly green hills. It is rather like parts of Somerset where the small green domes rise up, looking rather as if many buried St. Paul's had been sown with corn, oats and mustard'. Following in Morton's footsteps today it is easy to see how the county derived its name, Dunum, 'a hill or a hilly country.'

On the way out of Belfast along the A24, it is worth taking a short detour to visit the **Giant's Ring** which is an ideal place for a day trip and picnic. Little, if anything, is known about this striking prehistoric 600-feet-wide circular earthwork. Some scholars have suggested that it may have been a significant meeting place 2,000 years ago, but the exact purpose of the site is unclear. Remains from a Stone Age burial were discovered under the dolmen in the centre and during the eighteenth century, the ring was a popular venue for horse races. Nowadays, the Giant's Ring offers superb views of the parkland areas of South Belfast, as well as a purpose-built 2,000-year-old walking circuit around its edge.

There are two sites nearby which are worth a visit. **Drumbo**, from the Irish *Druim Bo* meaning 'ridge of the oxen', is a small village. It is laid out around a junction of routes converging at the front of the **Presbyterian church**, which is a listed building. The current church building is adjacent to the site of the medieval parish church, the foundations of which can be seen in the graveyard, as can the ruined lower half of a round tower. Also nearby is **St Patrick's Church of Ireland** in **Drumbeg** which is one of the best known landmarks of rural Belfast, due to the unusual stylish inclusion of the Lych Gate. It isn't known when the first church was built on this site but there was certainly a medieval church dating back to the thirteenth century. The site has been used by the Church of Ireland as a place of worship since the mid-seventeenth century. The church we see today dates back to

1870, but behind the church in the graveyard you can still see the remainder of walls from the original building. As well as featuring grandiose memorials to some of the wealthiest and most influential industrialists of the greater Belfast area, there are also simple headstones to foreigners such as the one commemorating two Norwegian seamen who were killed in an accident in the Belfast docks.

Back on the A24, the first major settlement in this part of County Down is the town of **Carryduff** which is six miles south of Belfast. The good road connections and its proximity to Belfast made the town an ideal site for overspill development from the city in the 1960s. This period saw numerous housing developments and shops. The original village formed where six roads and a river crossed, and is the site of the ancient Queen's Fort Rath, now sadly swallowed up. The A24 road from Belfast splits at Carryduff, one fork (A7) continuing to Downpatrick (via Saintfield and Crossgar), and the other fork (A24) continuing to Newcastle (via Ballynahinch). In addition, the road westwards from the Ards Peninsula, Newtownards, and Comber (now the B178) crosses here *en route* to Hillsborough in the west. All six roads cross the small Carryduff River here, which flows northwards to eventually join the River Lagan at Minnowburn.

The A7 from Carryduff takes you to the small town of **Saintfield**. Saintfield is set in the rolling hills of central Down, halfway between Belfast and Downpatrick.

Giant's Ring.

In recent years the town has developed as a service centre for the surrounding agricultural area, and is a growing commuter town. However, the architectural and historic significance of its town centre is reflected in its designation as a Conservation Area in 1997.

Saintfield, historically known as Tawnaghneeve, from the Irish *Tamhnach Naomh* meaning 'holy field', was settled during the plantation by James Hamilton, who had managed to secure a large portion of the land of Con O'Neill throughout north Down. In 1709, the estates were acquired by Major-General Nicholas Price whose mother was a Hamilton. On his new estate he began to establish the infant town of Saintfield, on which is now the west end of Main Street. In the early 1800s it improved rapidly and there was much employment in the weaving of linen. In his guide to County Down, published in 1886, Bassett wrote, 'On the last Wednesday of every month a fair is held. It is one of the best in the country for horses. Buyers attend from every part of the United Kingdom, and from France and Austria.'

Main Street contains, on the south side, a number of Georgian houses, many with modern adaptations. At Minnis's Corner you encounter the **First Presbyterian church**. The present church was built in 1777, although there was a Meeting House before that date. At the lower end of the graveyard many of the United Irishmen who were killed at the Battle of Saintfield in June 1798 were buried. Two of these graves are marked. On entering the vestibule of the church, visitors will find a tablet on the wall with its cautionary advice, 'Consider that ye here worship in the presence of him who seeth your actions and will shortly be your judge.'

The **Saintfield Church of Ireland** is in Main Street, right in the centre of town on the north side and has the graveyard surrounding it. The church was built in 1776, to replace an earlier church in Tonaghmore townland and repaired in 1812. There is an old stone set close to the door near the tower which reads 'Patrick vr9v'. According to tradition, it formed part of an older church and was placed in its present position to preserve it. It is said to come from the old church of Lisnegarric, one kilometre away, which was burned down in 1641 and which was dedicated to St Patrick.

A visit to Saintfield should include a stop at **Rowallane Garden**, which is a National Trust property, located just outside Saintfield. The garden was laid out from the mid-1860s by the Revd John Moore. Features include a walled garden, a natural rock garden wood, wildflower meadows, a farmland and a woodland walk, and a tearoom.

Saintfield is closely associated with the philosopher Francis Hutcheson who was born in Drumalig near the town. In 1729, he was appointed professor of

Far left: Church of Ireland Saintfield.

Left: Frances Hutcheson.

moral philosophy in the University of Glasgow, where he was one of the first academics to lecture in English rather than Latin. He was one of the leaders of the Scottish Enlightenment and an early utilitarian thinker, counting Adam Smith and Thomas Reid among his students. A plaque to Hutcheson is located at the **Guildhall** in the town.

Saintfield is probably most famous for the battle that took place there in June 1798, between the United Irishmen and the York fencibles, and local yeomanry during the Irish rebellion. A rebel force, over a thousand strong, converged on a large house owned by the McKee family. The McKees were a family of loyalists, who were unpopular in the region; one year before, they had provided information to the authorities leading to the arrest of a radical Presbyterian minister by the name of Birch and some members of his congregation. The McKees knew that they were unpopular and were armed to the teeth. As the house was surrounded, shots were fired from the fortified house, hitting some of the attackers. Gunfire held the insurgents back for a short while, until a fiddler by the name of Orr managed to sneak around the back of the house with a ladder, and set the roof alight. The house was destroyed, and all eight members of the family inside killed.

News of this quickly reached the British forces in the area, and a 300-strong force under Colonel Granville Staplyton, consisting of Newtownards Yeomanry cavalry and 270 York Fencibles, as well as two light cannon, marched to the region. The rebels, however, had anticipated the move and were waiting in ambush. Stapylton saw the road ahead twisting into woods, and ordered a pair of scouts to check for anything suspicious. The men do not seem to have been particularly vigilant, as when they returned, they declared that the road ahead was safe. The redcoats marched into the wooded area, a dense hedge snaking along the road on one side, and on the opposite side, the ground steadily rose, with the areas higher up the slope dominated by demesne woods. This provided cover for the rebels. The United Irishmen were mostly armed with pikes, and the terrain allowed them to quickly swarm the soldiers on the road below. In the fierce hand-to-hand combat that followed, the British forces were overwhelmed. One of the fencibles, a veteran of wars in Europe who managed to survive the attack, later stated that he had never before witnessed such fierce fighting, 'The soldiers were driven into disorder, and every man had to fight his way in the best manner he could in opposition to the charged pike and other weapons, to which he had not been accustomed.'

Over fifty men were piked to death, before Staplyton managed to rally the soldiers. He then brought his cannon into play against the mass of rebels before him, inflicting enough casualties with canister and grapeshot to blunt their attack. In the meantime, Staplyton's force used the confusion to march to safety. Over the following two days, the bodies were collected by the townspeople and buried in the hollow at a spot which has ever since been called York Island. Here in the 1950s, two skeletons and a sword and bayonet of the York fencibles were found in the area.

The A7 south of Saintfield takes you to **Crossgar**, from the Irish *an Chrois Ghearr* meaning 'the short cross'. There is a holy well known as St Mary's Well (*Tobar Mhuire*) which suggests that in this case *crois* (cross) is likely to refer to an ecclesiastical cross, no trace of which now remains. The **James Martin Memorial Stone** located in the Square in Crossgar is a tribute to the inventor of the ejector seat for aircraft who was born in the nearby townland of 'Killinchy-in-the-Woods' in 1893. Going west on the B7 you come to the **Ulster Wildlife Centre** at Crossgar. Here you can learn about wetland raised bog and meadowland flora and fauna.

The A24 takes the visitor from Carryduff to **Ballynahinch**. The rugged state of the countryside between Carryduff and Ballynahinch was confirmed by the historian Walter Harris in 1744 when he compiled his book *The Ancient and Present state of the County of Down*, in which he records:

> Ballinehinch is the principal, and almost only place of any note in the barony, and stands near the centre of the county on a little river. It lies in the midst of the great roads leading from Lurgan, Dromore, Lisburn and Hillsborough to Downpatrick and from thence to the eastern coast of the county. The country about is extremely coarse, full of rocks and hills, which render all access to it troublesome and unpleasant, and is justly complained of by travellers…

Visitors will be glad to know that the roads have considerably improved since Harris' time.

The name Ballynahinch, which comes from the Irish *Baile na hInse*, 'the town on the island', has often mystified observers who can see no trace of an island. The explanation for this is probably to be found in two factors: firstly, the low ground between the drumlin hills was a lot wetter in the past than it is now and, secondly, the word *Inse* has a secondary meaning of 'water-meadow' as well as the more common translation as 'island'.

At the beginning of the seventeenth century this part of mid-Down was McCartan's country, with the principal McCartan residence at Loughinisland, a

Left: Ballynahinch Town Centre.

Below left: Ballynahinch Junction in the 1930s.

Below right: Battle of Ballynahinch.

few miles to the south. In about 1660, Patrick McCartan sold the Ballynahinch area to Sir William Petty and Sir George Rawdon. After the Battle of the Boyne in 1690, more settled conditions encouraged immigration from lowland Scotland. Sir George Rawdon, whose descendants would become the Earls of Moira, had no love for the Presbyterianism that the settlers brought with them and thought them 'very troublesome … under pretence of their being godly men'.

Nevertheless, in succeeding centuries, Presbyterians formed the largest percentage of the population in the Ballynahinch district. This was an important factor in Ballynahinch's involvement in the 1798 Rebellion. Presbyterians were strongly attracted to the ideals of the United Irish movement after it was set up in Belfast in October 1791. Inspired by the French Revolution and with great admiration for the new democracy of the United States, the United Irishmen were led by Theobald Wolfe Tone, Thomas Russell, Henry Joy McCracken, and William Drennan. They came together to secure a reform of the Irish parliament, and they sought to achieve this goal by uniting Protestant, Catholic and Dissenter in Ireland into a single movement. This eventually led to rebellion in the summer of 1798.

During the 1798 Rebellion, Ballynahinch was the site of a significant battle. The insurgents were led by Henry Monro, a linen merchant in Lisburn and drill sergeant in the Lisburn Volunteers. He was a regular buyer at all the linen markets in Ulster, and as a result was well known as something of a dandy by all those in the linen markets. Upon hearing of the victory at Saintfield on 9 June, Monro joined the rebel camp there and then moved to Ednavady Hill, Ballynahinch to join the thousands who had gathered in support of the rebellion. The Revd Samuel Edgar, the Seceding minister in Ballynahinch, witnessed the dreadful preparation, 'Some were busy sharpening their pikes and preparing for battle; others, armed with these frightful weapons, were meeting me and crossing my path on their way to the camp. One stated the number in the camp to be 17,000.'

The response of the British garrisons was to converge on Ballynahinch from Belfast and Downpatrick in two columns, accompanied by several pieces of cannon. The insurgents took possession of Windmill Hill, at the north side of the town, and of the hill in the Moira demesne, now Montalto, at the south side, on the way to Dromara. General Nugent arrived on the 12 June from Belfast at the head of the Monaghan Militia, a detachment of the 22nd Dragoons, and some volunteer infantry and cavalry. Having met up with the forces of Colonel Stewart, who had advanced from Downpatrick, the entire force under his command numbered 1,500 men. An attack was made on Windmill Hill and resulted in its abandonment by the rebels. They joined their comrades in Moira demesne. Early on the following morning, the fighting was renewed for about three hours. At the entrance gate to the demense, the Monaghan Militia endeavoured to make a stand with two field pieces, but the rebel pikemen charged so furiously that they fell back in a state of demoralisation, upon the Hillsborough cavalry. In the meantime the Argyleshire fencibles were making an attack at another side of the hill, producing a diversion which allowed the Monaghan and Hillsborough contingents to rally. The rebels were ultimately routed and many fled into the surrounding countryside.

Ballynahinch was sacked by the victorious military after the battle, with sixty-three houses being burned down. Cavalry scoured the surrounding countryside for rebels, raiding homes and killing indiscriminately, the 22nd Dragoons being guilty of some of the worst atrocities. The one that lingered longest in popular memory was the killing of Elizabeth (Betsy) Gray, a young female rebel who, with her brother and fiancé, was slaughtered in the post-battle massacre. Betsy had gone on ahead and was taken first. When George Gray and Betsy's fiancé Willie Boad went to her aid they were shot down. Then a cavalryman called Jack Gill Nelson 'of the parish of Annahilt, aided by James Little of the same place', shot her through the head.

A nearby farmer found the bodies and buried them on his property. The murders created bad feelings among local families that lasted into the twentieth century and ensured her place in legend. She is the subject of many folk ballads and poems, including the following example written by the Victorian poet William McComb:

Now woe be on thee, Anahilt,
And woe be on the day,
When brother, lover, both were slain,
And with them, Bessie Gray.

In the nineteenth century, a member of the Gray family erected a monument at Ballycreen with the simple inscription 'Elizabeth Gray, George Gray, William Boad, 13th June 1798'. Sadly on the eve of the centenary of the rebellion the monument was destroyed by local Presbyterians who objected to the site being used by Nationalists to promote Irish independence.

The leader of the insurgents, Henry Monro, sought refuge at a farm owned by William Holmes, who betrayed them to the authorities. Monro was arrested by local yeomen and taken to Lisburn, where he was imprisoned. Monro was hanged on 16 June 1798 in the Market Square, Lisburn, within sight of his front door, with both his mother and one of his sisters looking on. According to an eyewitness, he settled his business accounts before ascending the gallows. His last words were 'tell my country I deserved better of her'. His head was cut off, impaled on a pike, and displayed for several weeks.

By the early nineteenth century, Ballynahinch had sufficiently recovered from the bloody events of 1798 to become a popular tourist centre, as visitors flocked to the town attracted by the medicinal qualities of the three wells at nearby **Spa**. The restorative properties of the water had been known since at least the early eighteenth century. Walter Harris, in his history of County Down in the 1740s, told the story of a Presbyterian clergyman afflicted with psoriasis and arthritis, who after spending a week at the Spa wells and drinking the waters, was soon cured and back to full health. The recommended regime for the waters was to drink between three and six pints per day. Harris described the taste as 'rich sulphureo-chalybeate spring of very clear water, and withal very cold; of disagreeable smell, resembling the waters of Aix-la-Chapelle, or the water used in scouring a foul gun' which 'Some it vomiteth, some it purgeth'.

Bramah pumps were installed at Spa Wells in 1810 by Mr David Ker of Montalto and a tourist boom occurred. In 1840, another member of the Ker family built a ballroom at Spa called the assembly rooms, now known as the Spa road-house. 'The season best adapted for restoring to Ballynahinch', wrote Dr Alexander Knox, in his *Irish Watering Places* published in 1845:

as to other medical springs, is from the middle of May to the end of September. At this period the water is in its greatest strength and purity, being undiluted by the rains of Winter, whilst the serenity of the weather and the joyous aspect of nature are alike favourable to that regularity of out-door exercise and cheerfulness of mind which prove such powerful adjuncts in effecting a cure. Patients who suffer much from heat and perspiration, and consequent liability to cold, will find the Spring and Autumn the most favourable periods for a visit to their favourite water-place.

Ballynahinch Spa.

Dr Knox recommended a course lasting three weeks or a month, 'a less period can be of little benefit'.

The railway, when it arrived in 1859, initially brought a flood of tourists from Belfast but ultimately led to a decline in Spa's fortunes, as Newcastle, with its sandy beaches and beautiful mountain scenery, was also were linked to the city of Belfast by rail. However, the tourist industry at Spa continued right up to the dawn of the Second World War. The industry adapted and catered for every whim of the tourists as it came along, providing croquet lawns and building a golf course, still thriving today.

Ballynahinch had benefitted greatly from the popularity of Spa, and by the 1880s Bassett describes it in his *Directory and Guide of County Down* as consisting of:

> a square and several streets. The houses are nearly all well built, and the places of business are well kept, and impress the stranger most favourably. Being situated in the centre of a first-rate agricultural country, a great portion of which has a limestone basis, the market for farm produce, held every Thursday, is stocked to repletion, and buyers are numerous. There is no town in the country where the market produces so complete a transformation from the routine of daily life. Every street has its scene of bustling activity, and in the Market Square, at some time of the day, all the energy is concentrated.

Since the 1950s the town has undergone the most rapid expansion in its history, due to the creation of many new housing estates. A reminder of former times can be seen in the **Market House** which was built in 1795 and is currently used by the community. According to local legend, Lord Moira was worried that his tenants would join the rebels in the event of a rising. In a bid to avert this, he called a meeting with them in the market house to address the issue. The tenants passed a resolution of loyalty to the Crown, vowing never to rise in rebellion. Moira was very proud of this achievement and appeared in the Irish House of Lords in February 1798 to assure the Lordships that there was no town more loyal than Ballynahinch. It was only a few months later that the tenants did indeed rise in rebellion, staging dramatic open warfare on Moira's own front lawn. This was of huge embarrassment to him and it is probably no coincidence that he sold the Ballynahinch estate shortly afterwards.

Five miles from Ballynahinch, is **Slieve Croob** ('the mountain of the hoof'), a bare and gaunt mountain, which is the source of the River Lagan which starts as a spring. The peak is lost in the maze of small country roads between Banbridge, Castlewellan, and Dromara. It is not a popular tourist destination, and not very well signposted, so to get there you will probably get lost two or three times on the way, even if you have a good map. Slieve Croob has been given the conservation designation Area of Outstanding Natural Beauty. According to local folklore, twelve kings are buried at the top of the mountain and each year it is traditional to climb the mountain on the last Sunday in August (known as Cairn Sunday or Blaeburry Sunday) and carry with you a stone to help bury the kings. In recent times, there has been traditional Irish music played at the top of the mountain on this date. It takes about thirty minutes at a moderate pace to walk to the top of the mountain. On a clear day the Galloway Coast of Scotland and the Isle of Man can be seen, and there are great views towards the Mournes and across Northern Ireland.

Legannany Dolmen, a prehistoric three-legged 'giant's grave' is located on the southern fringe of the Slieve Croob mountain range and offers stunning views of the Mourne Mountains. The tomb is over 1.5m high and the capstone is over 3m in length. Around the winter solstice the morning sun illuminates the entire underside of the capstone and tip of the backstone.

The B7 west from Ballynahinch takes you to **Dromara**, which was once a 'linen centre' with some 400 people employed in the local flax mills. The village was described by Lewis in his 1837 *Topographical Dictionary* as:

> ... a small village, partly in the barony of Kinelearty, partly in Lower Iveagh and chiefly in Upper Iveagh. It contains part of the lands granted by patent of Queen Elizabeth in 1585 to Ever Mac Rory Magennis which was forfeited in the war of 1641 and afterwards granted by King Charles II to Colonel Hill. They were included in the Manor of Kilwarlin.

Sadly the linen industry has long gone. St John's church, dating from 1811, is the oldest surviving building in Dromara, although the site of the church has a history extending back to the early fourteenth century as *Ecclesia de Druimberra*. It enjoys an upland setting, being located on the northern slopes of Slieve Croob. The River Lagan flows through the centre of the village and its valley dominates the landscape to the west of the village.

Nearby, there are a number of places of interest. **Finnis Souterrain** is known locally as **'Binders Cove'** which dates from the ninth century. Binder's Cove consists of a main passage of around 30m in length and two straight side passages on the right-hand side, each approximately 6m long. The passages are roughly 1m wide and 1.5m high. The walls are constructed of dry stone masonry and the roof comprises large flat stone lintels spanning between the walls. **Massford Tree** is a dead tree located in the middle of the village of Finnis, in which a bottle is hidden containing the exorcised spirit of an evil poltergeist. Some years ago, when either power lines or telephone lines were being run through the village, the tree stood in the way of progress and the priest had to be called to stop the workers from cutting it down. As a result they had to run the cables through the tree's upper branches.

Chapter 4

Downpatrick

Downpatrick, twenty-one miles from Belfast, is the county capital. Situated at the head of the picturesque Quoile Estuary, which opens into Strangford Lough, it lies irregularly in a valley surrounded by hills. Downpatrick is one of Ireland's most ancient and historic towns and is a good place to explore the surrounding countryside. It is also popular with horse-racing enthusiasts with **Downpatrick Racecourse**, where the first race meeting was held in 1685, located one mile from the town.

The town takes its name from a *dún* (fort), which once stood on the hill that dominates the town and on which Down Cathedral stands. Ptolemy, in about the year AD 130, includes it as *Dunum* in his list of towns of Ireland. The nucleus of the old town was in and around Rath Celtair, so called from 'Celtair of the Battles', one of the Red Branch knights who ruled the district about the beginning of the Christian era, and its earliest names was *Rath-Celtair-Mich-Duach*, or Dun Celtair 'the fort or house of Celtair'. He is described in the *Táin Bó Cúaligne* as 'an angry, terrific, hideous man, long-nosed, large-eared, apple-eyed, with coarse, dark, gray hair'. He was buried in the centre of the Rath, and an ancient Celtic cross for many years marked the spot of his burial, until it was removed by John de Courcy at the end of the twelfth century. The old name of the town was superseded by the name *Dun-leth-glas* which in turn gave way, in the thirteenth century, to the present name of *Dún Phádraig* (anglicised as Downpatrick) from the town's connection with the patron saint of Ireland.

It his difficult to imagine it today, but Downpatrick, for much of her history, was a seaside town. This ended in 1745 when the then landowner, Edward Southwell, erected the first tidal barrage across the Quoile, near the bridge on the old Belfast road. In 1957, a barrage was built further downstream at Hare Island, and this now controls all but the most severe of winter floods. Only the names Quoile Quay and Steamboat Quay survive as memories of the seafaring past, when Downpatrick was once a port with an extensive trade across the Irish Sea. The oldest buildings are to be found in English, Irish and Scotch Streets, on the hills which rose steeply above the waters of the inland sea. Newer buildings are located on Church and Market Streets, laid out on reclaimed land in 1838 and 1845 respectively. Even the traffic congestion, which occurs at the Town Hall Corner where the five principal main streets converge, is a daily reminder that this was the one dry-land connection between the oldest part of the town in English Street, and the main roads to Belfast and Dublin, which were its landward connection with the outside world.

The town was plundered on a number of occasions by the Danes. It was by this time ruled by the MacDunleavy clan, who probably had their headquarters on the Mound of Down. MacDunleavy dominance of the area ended with the arrival of an Anglo-Norman army in the late twelfth century. They arrived on the morning of 1 February 1177, led by John de Courcy with an army of Norman knights, Flemish crossbowmen and Welsh longbowmen. A contemporary description of de Courcy is provided by Gerald of Wales, who says, 'John was fair-haired and tall, with bony and sinewy limbs. His frame was lanky and he had a very strong physique, immense bodily strength, and an extraordinarily bold temperament'. Although brave, he was impetuous, 'and had about him the air of an ordinary soldier rather than that of a leader, yet away from the battlefield he was modest and restrained, and gave the church of Christ that honour which is its due.'

The Irish forces were no match for heavily armed knights on open ground. They faced a deadly rain of bolts and arrows, before they could get within range to use their shortbows and hurl their lances. According to Gerald of Wales in his *History and Topography of Ireland*, the Irish fought without arms:

> They regard weapons as a burden, and they think it brave and honourable to fight unarmed. They use, however, three types of weapons – short spears, two darts, and big axes and carefully forged, which they have taken over from the Northmen...They are quicker and more expert than any other people in throwing, when everything fails, stones as missiles, and such stones do great damage to the enemy in an engagement.

After a heroic struggle, the Irish forces, led by Rory MacDunleavy were defeated. According to Gerald of Wales:

> After an intense and for a long time indecisive struggle between these unevenly matched forces, John's courage at last won him the victory, and a great number of the enemy were killed along the sea shore where they had taken refuge. For because the surface

of the shore was soft and yielding, the weight of their bodies caused men to sink deep into it, and blood pouring from their wounds remained on the surface of the slippery ground and easily came up to their knees and legs of their pursuers.

An even greater Ulster coalition joined Rory MacDonleavy for a final attempt to oust the Norman in a great assault on Down in June 1177. Once again, the Norman forces triumphed and firmly established themselves in the Downpatrick area. Although there is no evidence that de Courcy himself was responsible for changing the town's name to Downpatrick, he did alter the dedication of Down Cathedral from the Holy Trinity to St Patrick, an act for which (according to the romanticized account of his exploits in the *Book of Howth*) God later took vengeance by denying him his Ulster lordship. De Courcy linked himself closely with the cult of St Patrick and commissioned *The life of St Patrick* by Jocelyn of Furness which was intended in part to prove the primacy of Armagh over Dublin.

For the next two centuries, the Anglo-Normans and Irish forces clashed at Downpatrick, and in 1315, Edward Bruce plundered and destroyed part of the town before proclaiming himself King of Ireland at the cross near the Cathedral. In May 1538, Lord Grey led a powerful army to enforce the spiritual supremacy of Henry VIII against the opposition raised by the wealthy abbots of this district, under Primate Cromer. Lord Grey defaced public monuments to the town's patron saints, and set fire to the Cathedral and the town. Three years afterwards, his actions in Downpatrick were included in the charges on which he was impeached and beheaded.

On the surrender of the abbey in 1539, its possessions, with those of the other religious establishments in the town, were granted to Gerald, 11th Earl of Kildare. In 1552, the town was plundered and partially destroyed by Con O'Neill, Earl of Tyrone; and two years afterwards it was assaulted by his son Shane, who destroyed its gates and ramparts. The town suffered further destruction during the rising of 1641, when those Protestants of the surrounding district who fled to the town for protection were slaughtered by an Irish under the command of Bryan O'Neill.

The town stubbornly re-emerged after each calamity to become the major administrative centre in the county in the eighteenth century. Lewis in his *Topographical Dictionary*, published in 1837, stated that Downpatrick:

consists of four principal streets rising with a steep ascent from the market-place in the centre, and intersected by several smaller streets and lanes: on the eastern side the hills rise abruptly behind it, commanding views of a fertile and well-cultivated tract abounding with richly diversified and picturesque scenery. It is divided according to ancient usage into three districts, called respectively the English, Irish, and Scottish quarters, and contains about 900 houses, most of which are well built: the streets are well paved, and were first lighted with oil in 1830; and the inhabitants are amply supplied with water ... The only article of manufacture is that of linen, principally yard wide, for the West Indies and the English market, and drills for Scotland, in which about 700 weavers, are employed.

St Patrick's Cathedral, Downpatrick.

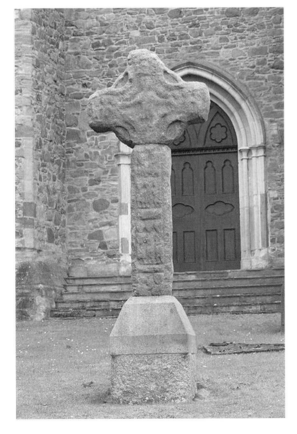

Above: St Patrick's grave.

Left: Celtic Cross.

By the late nineteenth century, the town was largely a market town, with industry on a much smaller scale. The most important feature of Downpatrick today is the Protestant Cathedral. The **Cathedral** crowning the height adjacent to the great Norman Mount in the marshes is an impressive site. It is a fragment of one of the only two purely Anglo-Norman churches in Ulster, the other being the Church of St Nicholas in Carrickfergus. It is believed to occupy the identical site of the monastery founded by St Patrick.

There is no actual mention of the monastery of Down in the *Irish Annals* until the year 583, when the death of Abbot Fergus is recorded. On eight occasions between the years 840 and 1103 this monastery was plundered by the Norsemen, the last raid being led by Magnus Barefoot, King of Norway. However on the way back to their ships the raiders were attacked and routed, and King Magnus himself was slain and buried at a spot that is still pointed out.

From then until the coming of de Courcy, Down was left in peace. De Courcy found in the old monastery a community of Canons Regular under the rule of St Augustine, but these he expelled and established in their place a Benedictine community which he handsomely endowed. For these Benedictines he built a magnificent abbey of which the present Cathedral is but the choir. Visitors to the Cathedral today must imagine that De Courcy's abbey was two and a half times longer.

It is generally accepted that the main walls of the Cathedral date from the years after 1220. Then the monks, in a petition to Henry III, King of England, referred to the fact that the House of St Patrick, which had often been destroyed and burned, was being rebuilt again. The Cathedral was successively destroyed in 1316 by Edward Bruce, and in 1538 by Lord Deputy Grey. In 1609, James I gave the Cathedral its chapter again, but the Cathedral was to lie in ruins for over 250 years, and during this period the parish church of Lisburn became the Cathedral Church of Down and Connor.

In 1790, restoration work began, but by that time only the chancel of the old Cathedral was left standing. The nave, transepts and cloisters had all been cleared away by anybody who chanced to need building materials, and even the round tower, of which a sixty-foot stump was left, was destroyed on the pretext that it might fall and damage the new building. The Cathedral today is, nevertheless, a striking building. The ten-pointed Gothic arches which divide the present nave from the side aisles are especially fine, the columns are massive and handsome, and the capitals beautifully carved. At the north-west corner of the nave is a capital carved with a series of female heads. The old font has an interesting history, for it was recovered from a farmyard where it was doing service as a horse-trough. Some say that this is the original Anglo-Norman font, but other experts are of opinion that it is of pure Celtic origin.

Most visitors head straight to the site where it is believed the bones of St Patrick lie in the shadow of the Cathedral. It was John de Courcy who, in 1185, took the remains of St Brigid, who died at Kildare in 523, and Columcille, who died in Iona in 597, and placed the three great saints of Ireland in one grave, giving rise to the well-known couplet:

> In Down, three saints one grave do fill,
> Patrick, Brigid, and Columcille.

St Patrick died in about the year 465, probably in the little village of Saul. From every monastery, monks with heads shaven from ear to ear set out to attend the obsequies. Great saints and scholars of the Celtic Church converged on Saul from every part of Ireland. For twelve days and nights the sound of chanting rose round the body of St Patrick. The night was as bright as day with the fire of torches. The Chiefs of Oriel demanded that the saint should be buried in Armagh; those of Ulidia demanded that he should lie in their capital of Dun-da-leth-glas, which became Downpatrick. It is ironic that is would be a Norman invader who would settle the argument, seven centuries later. In spite of rival claims from other places to be the saint's real burial ground, Downpatrick has been a pilgrims' centre of attraction for centuries.

Also worthy of a visit in the town is the ancient **Non-Subscribing Presbyterian church** which dates from 1711. One of the oldest Presbyterian churches in the province, the church has all its old fittings intact and is a fine example of its kind, with its pulpit high in the wall: the church is laid out in three wings, one in front of the minister, and one on each hand, each with a roomy gallery.

Downpatrick is notable for the number of museums. Going down the hill from the Cathedral, you can visit the fine **Down County Museum** which is housed in the old gaol. The gaol was opened in 1796 and, until its closure in 1830, housed many thousands of prisoners. It was built under the supervision of the Marquess of Downshire, the Earl of Hillsborough, the Hon. Edward Ward, and Charles Lilly, architect, between 1789 and 1796. The prison complex covers one acre and contains three main structures. These comprise a cell block to the rear, a central Governor's Residence, and two gatehouses flanking the main entrance, all set within a high perimeter wall.

In addition to incarcerating many people for very minor offences, the gaol held United Irishmen and rebels from the 1798 uprising, captured after the battles of Saintfield and Ballynahinch. It was in front of the old gaol that Thomas Russell, 'the

Man from God-knows-where', was executed for his role in the abortive rebellion of 1803. Thomas Russell is buried in the graveyard of the Anglican parish church of Downpatrick, **St Margaret's**, in a grave paid for by his great friend Mary Ann McCracken, sister of leading Belfast United Irishman Henry Joy McCracken.

The gaol was also a convict gaol and many hundreds of transportees were imprisoned here prior to their journey to the convict colonies of New South Wales. The museum began a programme of restoring the gaol buildings in 1981, and now visitors to the site can see the conditions in which the prisoners were kept, and visit restored cells complete with displays on individual prisoners. The museum's permanent exhibitions include 'Down Through Time' which explores 9,000 years of human history in County Down.

Down County
Museum.

Above: Downpatrick Jailhouse.

Left: St Patrick's Centre Downpatrick.

Across the road from the old gaol is the lovely group of Georgian buildings, which were erected as a **Southwell Blue Coat School** and Almshouses in 1733 by Edward Southwell, the benevolent landlord whose mother, the Lady Elizabeth Cromwell, was the only daughter and heiress of Vere Essex, 4th and last Earl of Ardglass.

The **Saint Patrick Centre** is an exciting interpretative exhibition which tells the fascinating story of Ireland's patron saint. Through Patrick's own words, a light is shone on the arrival of Christianity in Ireland and its development through his mission. A series of interactive displays allows visitors to explore how Patrick's legacy developed in early Christian times and reveals the fabulous artwork and metalwork which was produced during this Golden Age.

Until the Victorian era, Downpatrick was known for the difficulties visitors had in transversing its roads. The arrival of the railway in March 1859 transformed this situation. The *Downpatrick Recorder* summed up feelings in the area by declaring:

> It is gratifying to find that this railway is at length opened to the public. The first trip was made from Belfast to this town, on Wednesday morning, on one hour and 10 min-utes. This rate of speed is not to be expected on all occasions. The usual time likely to be taken, between the termini of the two towns, will be about an hour-and-a-half, which will be quite satisfactory to the public'.

As McComb described it, in his *Guide to Belfast* (1861) Downpatrick was now 'in communication with even remote portions of Ireland in consequence of the extension of railway intercourse. With Belfast it now maintains a regular and rapid interchange of passengers and merchandise; and from that central point tourists and commercial gentlemen have speedy access to the Southern, Midland, Western and North-Western towns and districts of the country, as well as, by steam navigation to the leading ports on the other side of the channel.'

Sadly trains would run into and through Downpatrick for less than a century. The line joined dozens of other branch lines across the province in the 1950s in the Department of Commerce and Production's rationalisation plan, which heralded the much of County Down's railway system. Rail enthusiasts should visit the local railway station which is home to Northern Ireland's only standard gauge (i.e. full-size) heritage railway. The **Belfast and County Down Railway** was founded in 1985, with the intention of rebuilding the entire former Belfast and County Down Railway branch line to Ardglass. However, it soon became apparent that this was an unrealistic goal and instead the railway was rebuilt to Inch Abbey and Ballydugan, both of which are on the former BCDR Belfast to Newcastle main line.

Within easy distance of Downpatrick, on a reach of the Quoile River, is the now preserved remains of the Cistercian Abbey of **Inch.** The site was originally on an island (*Inis* in Irish) in the Quoile Marshes. The pre-Norman Celtic monastic settlement here, known as *Inis Cumhscraigh* (or *Inis Cuscraidh*) was in existence by the year 800. In 1002, it was plundered by the Vikings led by Sitric, King of the Danes, who came up the Quoile with a fleet from the sea. The Vikings plundered the settlement again in 1149.

Inch Abbey was established as a Cistercian house by John de Courcy and his wife Affreca. Inch, or *Iniscourcy*, was erected as an act of repentance for the destruction of the Abbey at Erinagh three miles to the south by de Courcy in 1177. It was colonised directly by monks from Furness Abbey in Lancashire in 1180, along with some of the monks from Erinagh. The Cistercian monastery was located near to the river in the southern area of the early Christian earthwork enclosure. Monastic life continued, most likely on a small scale, until the sixteenth century. The Abbey was finally dissolved by 1541, when the Abbey, with about 850 acres of land, was granted to Gerald, Earl of Kildare.

The Cistercian precinct was enclosed by a bank and ditch, extending north and south from the parish graveyard to the river, and east to west up the valley sides. The buildings are mainly of the late twelfth and thirteenth century. The church was in the Cistercian cruciform plan with a low tower at the crossing, an aisled nave to the west, and two projecting transepts each with a pair of chapels. Only the impressive east window remains. On the stone plinth of the north transept's exterior north wall a number of incised symbols can be seen, which are masons' marks. The high altar was under the east windows and in the south wall are the remains of triple Sedalia (seats for the priests) and a piscina for washing the altar vessels.

Struell Wells is a set of four holy wells 1.5 miles east of Downpatrick. The wells date from before the time of St Patrick, and even today are used for people seeking cures. On Midsummer's Eve and the Friday before Lammas, hundreds of pilgrims used to visit Struell. The earliest written reference to the wells is in 1306, but none of the surviving buildings is earlier than about 1600. Mr and Mrs Hall, writing in the early 1840s, give the following account of the origin of the holy wells:

St Patrick and St Bridget were coming over the ground, and the younger saint, felling thirsty, doubted the capability of Patrick to procure her a drink as miraculously as Moses did for the Israelites. The latter then struck her on the foot with a wand which he held in his hand and a stream of blood issued forth, which was converted into water – which has remained so ever since.

Left: Woman's Bathhouse, Struell Well.

Below: Struell Well.

Remains of old church at Struell well.

By the beginning of the nineteenth century the Church was reasserting its authority by trying to stamp out irregular practices; this can be seen in *The Ordnance
Survey Memoirs* of the time. *The Ordnance Survey Memoirs* for the parish of Down,
written in 1836, noted that local people were in the habit of coming at certain
times of the year to Struell Wells and carrying off portions of the earth and stones
as preventatives of disease. These wells are located in the townland of Struell
and local people believed that St Patrick had endowed them with extraordinary
powers: one of the wells was said to restore sight to the blind. Until well into the
nineteenth century, people were said to gather in great numbers on St John's Eve
(23 July) to walk on bare knees across several heaps of stones placed in different
positions over the ground. They then made their way up a steep and stony portion
of rock known locally as St Patick's Chair, where a prayer was said. According to
the *Memoirs*, 'This practice has been rapidly declining of late years, it having been
forbidden by the clergy of the Roman Catholic Church.' It is perhaps not surprising that such a gathering provoked a hostile response from the church, for it was
custom for penitents to bathe in the wells at two specially constructed bath-houses.

'Even within the last 5 or 6 years the practice existed to an extant that appears extraordinary,' declares the *Memoirs*, 'and the bathing house…was seen filled by from 30 to 40 people of both sexes in a state of perfect nudity.' During the time that these ceremonies were going on, the ground in the neighbourhood used to be covered with tents for the sale of whiskey, and the Sunday after St John's Eve was devoted to all kinds of mirth and festival.

Nearby **Ballydugan Flour Mill**, on the Drumcullen Road, was built in 1792 by John Auchinleck of Strangford. It is six storeys high with two attics. It was fitted with a breastshot wheel, 6m diameter and 3m wide. There was also an auxiliary windmill. It was found that water from the Ballydugan Lake was only sufficient for eight months of the year and so a 25h.p. steam engine was later fitted. The mill contained four pairs of stones, two of them French burrs. The mill has been recently refurbished and is now a hotel and restaurant.

The **Quoile Pondage National Nature Reserve** is situated just outside Downpatrick on either side of the Quoile River. In an atmosphere reflecting the country cottage which stood here over 100 years ago, seasonal displays feature the unique nature of the Quoile Pondage and other nature reserves in County Down. The pondage is a 450-acre holding area for flood water from the river which is released through the barrage on the ebbing tide. A 2½-mile walk along the east bank of the River Quoile starts at a car park and picnic area near the Quoile Bridge. The walk takes visitors past the old sailing quays, and the skeleton of a coal schooner destroyed by fire in 1922. Further along is **Quoile Castle** is believed to have been built around 1600 and to have been associated with the West family. It has three floors below the attic and good barrel vaulting with wicker centering on the ground floor. Built on estuarine mud, the south-east angle eventually collapsed but has been conserved in its present state since the 1980s.

Ballydugan Mill.

The B1 south of Downpatrick takes you to **Ardglass** ('The Green Height'), which is famous for its herring fishery. Today Ardglass is the home port of thirty diesel-powered vessels, and is a major fish marketing and processing centre. Fish and prawns to the value of £4 or £5 million are landed in the port each year, most of it processed locally before shipping to the large cities of Europe.

Lewis's *Topographical Dictionary* left a memorable description of the place in 1837 when the habour was crowded with vessels:

> During the fishing season the view of the sea from this place is rendered peculiarly striking and animated by the daily arrival and departure of vessels and the numerous shoals of mackerel, pollock, and other fish visible on the surface of the water for miles. There are no manufactures; the labouring classes being wholly employed in the fisheries off the north-east coast, of which this place is the common centre. During the season there are frequently in the harbour, at one time, from 300 to 400 vessels from Donaghadee, Carlingford, Skerries, Dublin, Arklow, and the Isle of Man, but principally from Penzance, on the coast of Cornwall. The boats come regularly into the harbour to dispose of their fish, which is quickly purchased by carriers, who take it into the interior of the country, and by merchants who cure it; but chiefly by masters of sloops and small craft, who wait in the harbour for the arrival of the fishing boats, and proceed directly to Dublin or Liverpool to dispose of the herrings fresh.

Ardglass grew from a place of little note in the thirteenth century to an important town and port in the Middle Ages. It contains four medieval tower-houses, more than any other town in Ireland, reflecting its importance as Ulster's busiest port in the fifteenth century. It also has probably the most extensive network of warehouses from the period surviving in Ireland. These were important in the substantial grain export trade of the fourteenth and fifteenth centuries. Fortifications survive in the town from the fifteenth century, including Jordan's Castle, the most imposing of a ring of towers built around the harbour to secure the then important Anglo-Norman trading port, King's Castle and Cowd Castle.

Jordan's Castle is a castle situated close to the junction of Kildare and Quay Streets in Ardglass and commands the harbour. Its early history is somewhat obscure. The earliest authentic reference is to a defence of the castle against the O'Neills for three years by Simon Jordan, who for three years sustained the continued assaults of the besiegers, till he was at length relieved by the Lord-Deputy Mountjoy, who sailed with a fleet from Dublin and landed here on the 17 June 1601. It is a rectangular T tower house four storeys high, i.e. four superimposed single chambers each about 20ft by 13ft. On the north face, are two rectangular projections, one containing a stone spiral staircase, the other an inner closet at each level, with those on the lower stages having outlets to the ground.

King's Castle was originally built in the twelfth century and additions were made at various times over the centuries. It was rebuilt in the nineteenth century to the original specifications after parts of it collapsed in 1830 during repairs to the castle's foundation: restoration finished in 1988 and the castle opened as a nursing home and remains one today.

Margaret's Castle is a small tower house probably built in the fifteenth century. Only two storeys still exist but there is evidence that it was at least three storeys high. It is vaulted above the ground floor with a rectangular tower with projecting turrets in the north-west wall. The doorway between the turrets was protected by a murder-hole. A spiral stairway rises within the west turret. **Cowd Castle** is on the other side of the road from Margaret's Castle, at the entrance to Ardglass Golf Club. It is a small two-storey tower which may date from the late fifteenth century or early sixteenth century.

Of later vintage is **Ardglass Castle** which was converted from fortified warehouses at the harbour entrance that dated from the twelfth century after they were acquired by Charles Fitzgerald, 1st Baron Lecale in 1790. The castle and grounds were then bought by a group of local men wishing to start a golf club, and Ardglass Castle has been the golf clubhouse since then.

Nearby are the ruins of **Ardtole church** which overlooks the sea, half a mile to the north-east of Ardglass. The long narrow church seems to be of a fifteenth-century date, with a huge east window and opposing north and south doors, one with a draw-bar hole. In 1791, a cross-decorated slab of the early Christian period was found, showing that perhaps the site has a longer tradition than the surviving remains would suggest. According to local tradition some people from Ardglass found the chieftain of the MacCartans in a drunken sleep and fastened his hair to some briars. He avenged this affront with a massacre of the townsmen gathered together for Mass in Ardtole church. This disaster led to the abandonment of the building as a place of worship for Ardglass, probably in the sixteenth century.

Also worthy of a visit is nearby **Killough**. The village was originally known as St Anne's Port. The harbour was built in the eighteenth century by the Wards of Castle Ward House, just outside Strangford, which is why a notably straight road runs from Castle Ward to Killough. After the outbreak of war between Great Britain and France in 1793 the growing of cereals increased in Lecale, and Killough, as one of the ports of export, expanded to deal with it, until its population was almost double what it is today. For a brief period in the early nineteenth

Ardtole church, Ardglas.

Killough.

century, Killough was the busiest of the seaside villages of East Down and with its tree-lined main street, in many ways the most attractive. But when the post-war depression of the 1830s brought a fall in grain prices, merchants who had expanded in many fields during the inflationary period soon found themselves in difficulty.

According to G.H. Bassett in his *Directory and Guide to County Down* published in 1886, 'The principal feature of the village is one broad street, planted with shade trees, producing a most agreeable effect in the summer.' Today Killough has retained much of its charm and was designated a Conservation Area in 1981. It has a variety of listed buildings, including two churches, a number of private dwellings and the nearby listed Almshouses on the Rossglass Road, as well as an excellent beach.

Chapter 5

Newtownards and Strangford Lough

From Belfast city centre, cross the River Lagan by the Albert Bridge and into County Down along the A20 towards Newtownards. Just before you reach Dundonald, you will see the magnificent **Parliament Buildings** at Stormont. The need for a separate parliament building for Northern Ireland emerged with the creation of the Northern Irish Home Rule region in the Government of Ireland Act, 1920. It was opened by Edward, Prince of Wales (later King Edward VIII) on 16 November 1932.

The building is designed in the Greek Classical tradition in Portland stone, constructed by Stewart Partners Ltd under the guidance of architect Arnold Thornley, from Liverpool. The building stands at the top of the mile-long Prince of Wales Avenue. A statue to **Edward Carson** in dramatic pose (on the drive leading up to the building) is a rare example of a statue to a person being erected before their death. There is also a statue to Lord Craigavon, first Prime Minister of Northern Ireland, in the main foyer of Parliament Buildings, half way up the grand staircase. Craigavon and his wife are buried in the estate grounds. The surrounding parkland, with its sweeping city views, is open to the public and has marked paths and an excellent children's playground. In recent years, the grounds of Stormont have been used for more public-orientated functions such as an open-air concert venue, for acts such as Elton John, The Police and Rod Stewart, and the location for international sporting events.

A short distance away is **Stormont Castle**, a baronial mansion on the Stormont Estate in east Belfast, which is used as the main meeting place of the Northern Ireland Executive, following the restoration of devolved government. Between 1921 and 1972, it served as the official residence of the Prime Minister of Northern Ireland. In 1858, the Cleland family commissioned the local architect Thomas Turner to convert the existing Georgian house into a flamboyant baronial castle. The castle and grounds were acquired by the Northern Irish

Left: Parliament Buildings.

Below: Carson Statue, in front of Parliament Buildings.

Belfast Castle.

government in 1921. Until the restoration of devolution, Belfast Castle had served as the administrative Headquarters for successive secretaries of state.

Back on the A55 the next stop is **Dundonald**. The name refers to a twelfth-century Anglo-Norman fort, *Dún Dónaill*, that stood in the town. One of the largest in Ireland, the man-made hill that the fort stood on is still in existence. Until the 1960s, Dundonald was a small village. A number of property developments, most notably the housing estate Ballybeen, were then built and Dundonald's population rapidly grew. A 300-year-old watermill is located on the Belfast Road in the town. The sandstone building has been extensively restored and includes a brasserie, gift shop, and a thiry-five foot waterwheel, the largest in Ireland.

Ten miles from Belfast is the town of **Newtownards** at the head of Strangford Lough, which is surrounded by an amphitheatre of hills. The

Anglo-Normans founded a town in around 1226, named it *Nove Ville de Blathewyc* ('New Town of Blathewyc', the name of an earlier Irish territory) and established a Dominican priory. However, the town declined, and by the 1400s the land was controlled by the O'Neill clan, and the town lay virtually abandoned.

The medieval town declined along with the Norman colony, and was reduced to nothing more that a few mud-walled cabins and roofless buildings by the time Hugh Montgomery and other Scottish settlers arrived in the spring of 1606. He set about rebuilding what was by then known as Newtown, later expanded to Newtownards. He built a residence in the ruins of the old priory, the tower of which remains. Scottish settlers arrived in large numbers during the Plantation of Ulster and the town grew quickly. Due to the shallow mud of Strangford Lough, Newtown never developed as a port, with goods instead transported from the nearby town of Donaghadee. Newtownards became a market town, with the Market House in Conway Square constructed in 1770. The market still operates today on a weekly basis.

In the late eighteenth century, the town was redesigned with a new centre based around Conway Square, named after Alexander Stewart's daughter-in-law Lady Sarah Frances Seymour-Conway. New streets radiated north, south, east, and west, and were named after these compass points. The early nineteenth century, saw the reclamation of the marshlands south of the town. Regent Street, became the main avenue through the town as it continued to expand throughout the nineteenth century. Commercial premises such as factories, shops and banks were built, serving the needs of the townspeople and those in the surrounding countryside. New streets were also laid out to house handloom weavers and other mill workers. According to Lewis's *Topographical Dictionary* in 1837:

> The first attempt to establish a public brewery, and also a public distillery, was made in this town in 1769; but both failed, and, in 1819, John Johnston, Esq., purchased the premises and rebuilt the brewery on an extensive scale; more than 7,000 barrels of beer are brewed annually, and adjoining are large malting premises for the supply of the brewery and for sale, in which the malt is made from barley grown in the neighbourhood. The weaving of damask is carried on to a small extent; about 600 looms are employed in weaving muslin, and 20 in weaving coarse linen for domestic use. More than 1,000 females are constantly employed in embroidering muslin for the Glasgow merchants, who send the fabrics hither for that purpose.

Above: Newtownards Priory.

Left: Newtownards Old Cross.

Below: Newtownards Town Hall.

Newtownards acquired rail links to Belfast via Comber and Dundonald in 1850 and to Donaghadee in 1861. By the same year the town's population had risen to 9,500. As the economy became increasingly tied to Belfast, the town continued to prosper, and by the twentieth century had increasingly become a commuter town.

Newtownards has the only surviving seventeenth-century **market cross** in Northern Ireland. The edifice, which stands at the east end of High Street, is an octagonal monument, originally built in 1636. **St Mark's church** was constructed of Scrabo stone in 1817. The building is a good example of planters' gothic architecture. The Londonderry family contributed generously to the cost of St Mark's and their family crest is carved above the west door. The weavers of Newtownards contributed a rose window in 1868.

Blair Mayne Statue.

The **Dominican Priory** was founded in 1244 by the Savage family. Known as the Black Priory, owing to the black mantle worn over the white habit, the Dominicans were a mendicant order. The priory was destroyed by the O'Neills in 1572 to prevent Queen Elizabeth I from planting an English settlement. It was later used as a parish church until St Mark's opened in 1817.

A lifesize bronze statue of **Blair Mayne** stands in Conway Square and the western bypass of the town is also named in his honour. He was capped six times by the Irish Rugby team before the outbreak of the Second World War. He won the Irish universities heavyweight boxing championship in 1936 and the Scrabo Golf Club's Presidents Cup the following year. His sporting life, however, was overshadowed by his brilliant military career in which he went from a Newtownards Territorial Army recruit to founder member of the much feared SAS, the British Army's ultimate fighting force. He was awarded the DSO, the second highest medal for gallantry, four times, and the Croix de Guerre. He died at the early age of forty in 1955 in a car accident near his home in Newtownards.

The **Town Hall** is steeped in history. The ground floor of the building was the **Market House** for local traders. There was also a 'lock-up' cell with grilled windows around which were grooves reputed to have been made by the fingers of prisoners. The upper story held an assembly room. The Market House was seized by the United Irishmen on their way to the Battle of Saintfield, during the 1798 Rebellion. Rebels were later rounded up and imprisoned in the cells below the Market House, to await judgment and execution.

Situated one mile east of Newtownards, on the south of the B172 to Millisle, lie the ruins of **Movilla Abbey** which was one of Ireland's most important monasteries. It was founded in AD 545 by St Finian who named it *Movilla* (*Magh Bile*, 'the plain of the sacred tree', in Irish) which suggests that the land had previously been a sacred pagan site. This monastery was destroyed by the Vikings sometime after 824, and in the twelfth century joined together with Bangor Abbey as an Augustinian Monastery. Later, the monastery was raided by Hugh O'Neill from mid-Ulster, after which the urban settlement at Movilla disappeared and the area around it became known as Ballylisnevin, 'the town land of the fort of the family of Nevin'. The graveyard contains many old graves, as well as the more modern ones, including that of Colonel Paddy Mayne.

The town of Newtownards is overlooked by the 100-foot-high **Scrabo Tower**. The landmark, which is visible from most of north Down, was built on a volcanic plug above the town in 1857 as a memorial to Charles Stewart, 3rd Marquess of Londonderry who was one of the Duke of Wellington's generals during the Napoleonic Wars, in recognition of his concern for the plight of his tenants during the great potato famine. An inscribed stone panel may be seen above the doorway on the north side. The inscription reads:

Erected in memory of Charles William Vane,
3rd Marquis of Londonderry KG and C by his tenantry and friends
Fame belongs to history, remembrance to us 1857

The tower was built to designs attributed to Charles Lanyon and W. H. Lynn, and now stands in a country park. The park has several woodland walks and parkland through Killynether Wood. The view from the hill and the summit of the tower extends across Strangford Lough, scattered with its many islands, to the Mountains of Mourne and the Scottish coast. The tower houses two floors of displays and a climb of 122 steps takes the visitor to the open viewing level. **Scrabo Country Park** is always open admission to the park and the tower is free.

The **Somme Heritage Centre** is situated a little north of the town. Located adjacent to the Clandeboye Estate outside Newtownards, the centre is a unique visitor attraction of international significance showing the awful reality of the Great War and its effects on the community at home. The centre commemorates the involvement of the 36th Ulster and 16th Irish Divisions in the Battle of the Somme, the 10th Irish Division in Gallipoli, Salonika and Palestine, and provides displays and information on the entire Irish contribution to the First World War. Historically, the 36th (Ulster) Division trained over the Estate during the first few months of the war, and German Prisoners of War were interned there.

Heading south-west from Newtownards, the small town of **Comber** (from the Irish *An Comar* meaning 'the confluence') is situated at the northern end of Strangford Lough. The confluence of two rivers, which gave the town its name, is that of the Glen River and the Enler River, which meet here. There is believed to have been a church here since the time of St Patrick, while a Cistercian Abbey was founded in around 1200 on the site of the present Church of Ireland, a site likely chosen to take advantage of the good access to Strangford Lough. After Henry VIII dissolved the monasteries in 1541, the abbey fell into ruins and its stone has since been used in other buildings.

During the influx of Scots in the early 1600s, settlement grew at Comber, although it was focused about a mile further south than at present, in the townland of Cattogs, and there is evidence that the settlement was a port used by traders and fishermen. By the 1700s, however, the focus of the town had moved to the area of the present Main Square and Comber became established as an industrial centre with several mills.

The Andrews family made Comber a centre of both linen production and grain processing by the second half of the eighteenth century. Whiskey distilling was a prominent industry by the mid-1800s, the most prominent of the distillers being John Miller. Many members of the Andrews family have risen to positions of distinction. One such was **John Miller Andrews**, Prime Minister of Northern Ireland. He was an enthusiastic opponent of Irish Home Rule and threw himself wholeheartedly into Ulster Unionist opposition to a Dublin Parliament. As one of the architects of Northern Ireland, he sat in its parliament for County Down (1921-9) and then for mid-Down and County Down from 1930, and held high office for over twenty years, as successively minister of labour (1921-37), minister of finance (1937-40), and finally Prime Minister (1940-43).

Another member of the Andrews family who rose to fame was **Thomas Andrews**, the designer of the ill-fated *Titanic*. Andrews headed a group of Harland & Wolff workers who went on the maiden voyages of the ships built by the company, to observe ship operations and spot any necessary improvements. The *Titanic* was no exception, so Andrews and the rest of his Harland & Wolff group travelled from Belfast to Southampton on *Titanic* for the beginning of her maiden voyage on 10 April 1912. During the voyage, Andrews took notes on various improvements he felt were needed. However, on 14 April, Andrews remarked to a friend that *Titanic* was 'as nearly perfect as human brains can make her'.

Later than evening, Andrews lost his life when the ship struck an iceberg and sank. As the evacuation of the *Titanic* began, Andrews searched the staterooms, telling the passengers to put on lifebelts and go up on deck. Fully aware of the short time the ship had left, and of the lack of lifeboat space for all passengers and crew, he continued to urge reluctant people into the lifeboats in the hope of filling them as fully as possible. According to John Stewart, a steward on the ship, Andrews was last seen staring at a painting, *Plymouth Harbour*, above the fireplace in the first–class smoking room. Newspaper accounts of the disaster labelled Andrews a hero. Mary Sloan, a stewardess on the ship, who Andrews persuaded to enter a lifeboat, later wrote in a letter, 'Mr. Andrews met his fate like a true hero, realizing the great danger, and gave up his life to save the women and children of the *Titanic*. They will find it hard to replace him.'

Comber boasts one of the earliest and most substantial memorials for a single victim of the *Titanic* disaster. The **Thomas Andrews Jr Memorial Hall** was opened in January 1914. The architects were Young and McKenzie, with sculpted work by the artist Sophia Praegar. The hall is now maintained by the South Eastern Education Board and used by the Andrews Memorial Primary School.

Far Left: Thomas
Andrews.

Left: Statue of Robert
Rollo Gillespie.

The twentieth century saw Comber lose much of its industry but re-establish itself as a commuter town for the Belfast urban area. Comber's main square has a statue of 'Rollicking Rollo', **Sir Robert Rollo Gillespie** (1766-1814), born in a large house on the south side of the square. A fiery character, he joined the 3rd Irish Horse as a Cornet. He was involved in a duel, fled to Scotland, but then returned voluntarily to stand trial in 1788. The verdict was 'justifiable homicide'. He then joined the Jamaica Light Dragoons, and was Adjutant-General of St Domingo when eight men broke into his house. Armed only with his sword, Gillespie killed six of them and the other two fled. After a series of thrilling adventures, Gillespie led a column to attack a Nepalese hill fort at Kalunga in 1814 at the beginning of the Gurkha War. The Gurkhas launched a sortie which was repulsed. Gillespie tried to follow them back into the fort with a dismounted party of the 8th Dragoons. Although this failed, Gillespie renewed the attack with companies of the 53rd Foot. He was trying to rally these men, just thirty yards from the fort when a Gurkha sharpshooter shot him through the heart. Without him, the attack collapsed.

The statue of Major-General Sir Rollo Gillespie was constructed under the oversight of John Fraser, the first County Surveyor of Down, and was unveiled on 4 June 1845 in the Town Square of Comber. Fifty lodges of the Masonic Order were present, in what is believed to be the biggest Masonic gathering in Irish history. It was calculated that 25,000 to 30,000 people crowded into the town to witness the ceremony. The column is fifty-five feet high. At the foot of the column are many Masonic symbols and his famous last words, 'One shot more for the honour of Down.'

From Comber, we follow the west shore of Strangford Lough, a district as rich in the ruins of castles and churches. The name **Strangford Lough** comes from the Old Norse *Strangrfjörthr* meaning 'strong ford', describing the fast-flowing narrows. In Irish it is called *Loch Cuan* meaning 'calm lough', describing the still shallow waters of the mud flats. It is a popular tourist attraction, noted for its fishing and the picturesque villages and townships which border its waters.

In the folklore of Strangford Lough, poetically named as 'Loch Cuan of the Curraghs', the story is told that the Irish sea god Manannan Mac Lir, in a grief-induced rage over the killing of his son, let forth an outburst of water which formed three Irish sea loughs: Waterford, Dundrum Bay, and Strangford Lough. Strangford is a place of outstanding natural beauty. It has a dramatic rocky shoreline to the south, drumlins to the west, and bird-trodden mud flats to the north, as well as islands, shallow reefs, bays, headlands, and marches. Vast quantities of microscopic plankton are swept into the lough every day which provides a ready food supply for an enormous range of creatures, making it one of the richest places for maritime life in the whole of Europe. Occasionally, a massive basking shark, the world's second largest fish, is spotted cruising around the entrance of the lough, feasting on plankton. In September, flocks of pale-bellied brent geese arrive from Arctic Canada, while wigeons make the journey from Iceland and Russia. With so many small islands and a plentiful food supply, Strangford Lough is an ideal nesting site for up to forty different species of birds.

The lough has attracted visitors for centuries, from prehistoric settlers who hunted wildfowl in its marshes and woods, to the Vikings who lived near the lough for over 200 years from the ninth century. One such was Magnus Barefoot, King of Norway, nicknamed 'Barelegs', who was killed in battle near Downpatrick in the year 1103. Today's visitors are attracted by bird-watching tours, boats for hire and excellent viewpoints of the wildlife all around the lough.

Strangford Lough.

Travelling south from Comber, it is well worth a detour to visit **Mahee Island** which is approached along a narrow, twisting causeway signposted off the main A22. It is the location of **Nendrum Monastery**, founded in the fifth century by St Machaoi. A small Benedictine cell was later founded in the late twelfth century. It was a parish church in 1306, but abandoned during the fifteenth century. **Mahee Castle**, also known as Nendrum Castle, is a ruined tower house on Mahee Island. The entrance doorway is on the north-west end, defended by a murder-hole inside. It has two ground-floor rooms, the larger with a semicircular vault built on plank centering and the smaller with a pointed vault.

South along the A22, turn off onto the Beachvale Road to the village of **Killinchy** (from the Irish *Cill Dhuinsí* meaning '(Saint) Duinseach's church') which is two miles inland from the western shores of Strangford Lough. The village is a good place to appreciate the majesty of Strangford Lough. 'I shall never forget the sight of this lough from a high hill near Killinchy', wrote H.V. Morton in 1930:

> The salt water was stirred by a sea wind. The edges of the lough were fringed with that glorious golden weed called by Western Islesmen in Scotland femin fearnaich (I cannot guarantee the spelling), a weed full of iodine, from which, I image, the ancient Irish obtained the saffron dye for the kilt. The near bank of the loch was dotted with small green islands which looked as though the children of the hills of Down were playing in the water. These miniature hills lifted their green domes out of the green sea water and some of them were sown in vertical strips with different root crops, strips of bright mustard-yellow would alternate with squares of golden wheat or the dark green of beet. The gulls circled over the water and stood in white companies in the yellow weed on the shores of these fairy islands. Strangford Lough is Ulster's Killarney.

There are two archaeological sites within the village limit: the church to the north and the windmill stump to the south. **Killinchy Presbyterian church** is a traditional country church with a rich history of Christian worship and witness dating back to 1630. The original Meeting House, erected in 1670, was replaced on a number of occasions before the present church was built in 1739. It is one of the few cruciform churches to be found in Ireland. A couple of miles from Killinchy is **Sketrick Castle** which is situated on the western extremity of Sketrick Island. Now joined to the mainland by a causeway, there is a raised footpath from the mainland and the strait of water separating the two is nearly dry at low tide.

South again on the A22 is the large village of **Killyleagh** (from the Irish *Cill Uí Laoch* meaning 'church of the hero's descendants'). Killyleagh was settled in the twelfth century by John de Courcy, who built fortifications on the site of the castle in 1180, as part of a series of fortifications around Strangford Lough for protection from the Vikings. In 1602, Gaelic Chieftain Con O'Neill of Clandeboye owned large tracts of North Down, including Killyleagh. O'Neill sent his men to attack English soldiers after a quarrel and was consequently imprisoned. O'Neill's wife made a deal with Scots aristocrat Hugh Montgomery to give him half of O'Neill's lands if Montgomery could get a royal pardon for O'Neill. Montgomery obtained the pardon but King James I divided the land in three, with the area from Killyleagh to Bangor going to another Scot, James Hamilton, later 1st Viscount Cladeboye.

The location of a good anchorage brought trade and prosperity to the growing town of Killyleagh. It was designated a Maritime Port in 1620 and a stout harbour was built. This also led to the expansion of the fishing industry. A cotton mill was built at the end of the eighteenth century and soon, at Shrigley, Martin's great flax spinning mill was erected, which became on of the largest in Ireland.

The waterfront is still the focal point of the town and growing interest in tourism and small-boat sailing have been fostered not least by the appointment of Prince Andrew as Baron Killyleagh in 1986. His visits after his marriage and latterly to unveil the **Sir Hans Sloane** statue have helped to highlight this small and busy town, which is surrounded by the beautiful scenery of Strangford Lough with the backdrop of the fairytale castle.

Above left: Sketrick Castle.

Above right: Killyleagh, 1900.

Sloan Statue, Killyleagh.

Killyleagh Castle dominates the small village and is believed to be the oldest inhabited castle in the country, with parts dating back to 1180. It is currently the home of Gawn Rowan Hamilton and his young family. The castle hosts occasional concerts, while the gate lodges provide self-catering holiday accommodation.

A map of Killyleagh from 1625 shows the castle as having a single tower on the south side of a residence. In about 1625, Hamilton moved from Bangor to Killyleagh Castle, where he built the courtyard walls. Viscount Claneboye's son James Hamilton, 1st Earl of Clanbrassil, built the second tower. He supported the Stuart monarch Charles I of England and the castle was besieged in 1649 by Oliver Cromwell's forces, who sailed gunboats into Strangford Lough and blew up the gatehouse. The Earl fled, leaving behind his wife and children. Parliament fined him for the return of the castle and his land. The 1st Earl's son Henry Hamilton, 2nd Earl of Clanbrassil, rebuilt the castle in 1666. He erected the north tower and built (or perhaps restored) the long fortified bawn (wall) in the front of the castle.

Far left:
Killyleagh
Castle.

Left: Lady
Dufferin.

Lady Dufferin wrote a number of poems and songs while staying at Killyleagh Castle, including the *Lament of the Irish Emigrant*:

I'm biddin' you a long farewell,
My Mary – kind and true!
But I'll not forget you, darling!
In the land I'm goin' to;
They say there's bread and work for all,
And the sun shines always there,
But I'll not forget old Ireland,
Were it's fifty times as fair!

And often in those grand old woods
I'll sit, and shut my eyes,
And my heart will travel back again
To the place where Mary lies;
And I'll think I see the little stile
Where we sat side by side:
And the springin' corn, and the bright May morn,
When first you were my bride.

Killyleagh parish church is on top of Church Hill, overlooking the harbour and Strangford Lough. It was built in 1640 by Viscount Clandeboye. The church was built in the cruciform shape, but the addition of the aisle, where the font now stands, and the vestry, spoils the cruciform. The architecture is Jacobean. It fell into a bad state of repair and was rebuilt in 1812, at the expense of £2,000, by James, 2nd Baron Dufferin and Clandeboye, to whom a monument is erected on the east wall of the south transept. The roof was raised and a tower and spire added in 1824. The 'old line' of the roof can still be seen under the present plaster of the painted interior.

There are eight memorial windows, including one to the memory of **Revd Edward Hincks** who was rector of the church from 1822 until 1866. Hincks, a renowned Assyriologist and Egyptologist, was one of the first to decipher Egyptian Hieroglyphics and Ancient Persian Script. The undemanding nature of his clerical duties left him with more than enough time to pursue his interest in ancient languages. His first love was for the hieroglyphic writing of ancient Egypt. By 1823, the Frenchman Jean-François Champollion had succeeded in deciphering this enigmatic script, but Hincks made a number of discoveries of his own which established him as an authority of ancient philology. Stories are told of Hincks preaching at church on a Sunday and then disappearing from the pulpit in the middle of a sermon. As he preached, he sometimes managed to complete something he had been deciphering earlier and had to retire to the adjoining rectory to write it down before he forgot it. Afterwards, he would return to his awaiting congregation to complete the sermon.

Although Hincks is recognised now, in his time he did not receive the acclaim he deserved for his genius. Hincks was disappointed at the lack of public recognition of his achievements in Britain, and his failure to obtain a more financially secure position to allow him to devote more time to his studies. However, following his death on 3 December 1866 aged seventy-four, Professor Maspero, Director of the Museum in Cairo, commissioned a marble bust as a lasting tribute to the contribution Dr Hincks had made to the knowledge about Ancient Egypt. A portrait of him hangs in the Manuscript Reading Room, Trinity College as a memorial of the institution's brilliant scholar.

The other notable family buried here is that of **Sir Hans Sloane**, the distinguished physician and collector, remembered today for bequeathing his collection to the British nation, which became the foundation of the British Museum. Such was his eminence that he gave his name to Sloane Square in London, as well as Sir Hans Slone Square in his birthplace, Killyleagh, where a statue of him can be found near the habour.

By November 1694, Sloane had risen to the position of physician in charge of Christ's Hospital, London, a post he held until 1730. With a generosity that was also characteristic of him, he returned his salary of £30 a year to the hospital on a regular basis for the relief of needy inmates. Further recognition of his medical prowess came in 1712 with an appointment as physician-extraordinary to Queen Anne. In 1714, he attended the Queen in her final illness. De Beer draws attention to the crucial significance of Sloane's role in prolonging the Queen's life to the point where the succession of the Protestant George I could be ensured, so thwarting Jacobite aspirations to regain the throne. Under George I, Sloane continued to serve as a physician-extraordinary and on 3 April 1716, shortly after the King's accession, he was created a baronet, one of the first physicians to be so honoured. A court appointment followed in the succeeding reign when, in 1727, Sloane became physician-in-ordinary to George II, 'having been before constantly employ'd about the whole Royal Family, & always honour'd with the Esteem & favour of the Queen Consort'.

After Killeagh you head towards Downpatrick, but on the outskirts of the town take the A25 towards Strangford. A few miles out of Downpatrick is the village of **Saul** (from the Irish *Sabhall* meaning 'barn'). **Saul church**, a replica of an early church with a round tower, is built on the reputed spot of St Patrick's first sermon and church in Ireland. When St Patrick came to Ireland in 432, strong currents swept his boat through the Strangford Lough tidal narrows and he landed where the Slaney River flows into the lough. The local chieftain, Dichu, was quickly converted and gave him a barn for holding services.

St Patrick is said to have died in Saul on 17 March 461. Close by, on the crest of Slieve Patrick Hill is a massive statue of Patrick where bronze panels illustrate scenes from his life. According to the eighth-century hymn of St Fiacc, Patrick received his last communion from St Tassach. You can see the ruins of **St Tassach's church**, one of Ireland's earliest Christian buildings, at Raholp near Saul.

Edward Hincks.

Making your way back to the A25 a few miles will take you to the pretty village of **Strangford**. Strangford is situated across Strangford Lough from Portaferry and is the main base for the Strangford Lough ferry service. No fewer than five small castles are within reach of Strangford, testifying to its strategic importance: these are Strangford Castle, Old Castle Ward, Audley's Castle, Walshestown, and Kilclief. The village has a small harbour, which is overlooked by rows of nineteenth-century cottages and a fine Georgian terrace.

Strangford Castle, located near the harbour in Strangford, is a sixteenth-century tower house with drop hole at roof level to defend the door. It appears to be a small tower house from the late sixteenth century, but a blocked door of fifteenth-century type at first-floor level, seems to indicate the remodelling of an earlier tower. The current entrance, in the north-east wall, is a reconstruction, positioned by the surviving corbelled machicolation above and a socket from a draw-bar to secure the original door. The original entrance may have been on the first floor. It is a small, rectangular, three-storey tower house with no vault or stone stairway. The first-floor fireplace has an oven. The ground-floor chamber is lit only by small gun-loops. The roof has very fine crenellations, again with pistol-loops. The original floors, like their modern replacements, were made of wood.

Above left: Saul church.

Above right: Stained glass in Saul church.

© Brian T McElherron

Audley Castle.

A few miles north of Strangford is the imposing **Castle Ward**, owned by the National Trust. Overlooking the south shores of Strangford Lough, Castle Ward is one of Northern Ireland's finest demesnes or country estates. Castle Ward's most interesting aspect is that of its dual architecture. While the entrance side of the building is done in classical style, the opposite side is distinctly Gothic. This curious arrangement reflects the disagreement between the 1st Lord Bangor, Bernard Ward, and his wife, for whom the house was built in the 1760s. He favoured the classical style and she preferred the Gothic. This duality in style continues throughout the house with the divide down the centre. The classical columns and door cases contrast with Gothic rooms, such as the boudoir with an extravagant fan-vaulted ceiling, modelled on Henry VII's chapel in Westminster Abbey.

Audley's Castle, a few miles south of Castle Ward, is a fifteenth-century castle located on a rocky height overlooking Strangford Lough. Audley's Castle consists of a tower set within a yard (technically known as a bawn) which is enclosed by a thin wall, with a simple gate. It is protected on its south side by a rocky cliff. The stone walls of the bawn have been reduced to low foundations, but its rectangular plan can still be traced. The south-east face of the tower house is dominated by two projecting square turrets, linked by an arch at parapet level (a machicolation), through which objects could be dropped on anyone attacking the door in the south turret below. The ground-floor room is entered through a small lobby which has a murder-hole in its roof. The south turret contains a spiral stair which leads to the two upper chambers and the roof.

Chapter 6

North-West Down

Near to Banbridge Town, in the County Down
One morning in July,
Down a boreen green came a sweet colleen,
And she smiled as she passed me by;
Oh, she looked so neat from her two white feet
To the sheen of her nut-brown hair,
Sure the coaxing elf, I'd to shake myself
To make sure I was standing there

Oh, from Bantry Bay up to Derry Quay,
And from Galway to Dublin town,
No maid I've seen like the brown colleen
That I met in the County Down.

The Star of County Down

The MI west out of Belfast passes south of the city of Lisburn and north of the village of Moira. Lisburn, the third largest city in Northern Ireland, is situated on the River Lagan with the vast majority of the city north of the river in County Antrim. With its fine Irish Linen Centre, Christchurch Cathedral and bustling shops and restaurants, it is a good place to explore the often neglected north-western part of County Down.

Four miles south of Lisburn is the pretty village of **Hillsborough**. The historic centre of the village contains a significant amount of Georgian architecture. It was the property of the Hill (later Downshire) family, which owned 64,356 acres in County Down, representing around half their Irish lands. The Downshire estates included a number of urban settlements such as Banbridge, Hilltown, Dromara, Loughbrickland, and Hillsborough became the capital of these vast estates. In October 1771, Benjamin Franklin spent five days in Hillsborough as the guest of Willis Hill, Secretary of State for the colonies. The animosity that developed between the two men would contribute to the American War of Independence.

Hillsborough was known before the Plantation of Ulster as Cromlin, from the Irish *Cromghlinn* meaning 'crooked glen', where it was the location of a fortified farmhouse owned by the Maginneses and the ruins of an ancient chapel dedicated to Saint Malachi. In 1611, Moyses Hill, a former soldier who had served in Ireland, gained possession of Cromlin from the Maginneses. It was a shrewd investment: his descendants would become among the richest and most influential landlords in Ireland.

In about 1630, his son Peter Hill began the construction of a village and fort commanding the pass on the main highway from Carrickfergus to Belfast. The place was destroyed during the Irish rising of 1641 and it was left to Peter's uncle and heir, Sir Arthur Hill to restore the village's fortunes. He built **Hillsborough Fort** in 1650, which stands on the site of an Early Christian period rath, the circular ditch of which has been left open in the central grassed area of the fort. In 1690, William of Orange stayed four nights at Hillsborough Fort, on his way to the Boyne. A tablet at the entrance gate records that before departure he gave a grant to the clergy of the Presbyterian Church in acknowledgment of their support. He also gave a yearly grant of king's plate to the Down Royal Corporation of Horse Breeders, whose **Maze Race Course** still lies about a mile and a half from the town.

These days, it is possible to walk around the battlements and square corner towers, and from the rampart at the back of the Fort, one can look across a beautiful lake, artificially constructed at the end of the eighteenth century and known as the **Large Park**. The lake is situated in **Hillsborough Forest**, a large park with scenic wooded parkland, forest walks and lakeside paths. It is a very popular centre for family picnics and walks.

On the south-west of the Market Square is **Hillsborough Castle**, which is in fact a Georgian mansion built in the eighteenth century for the Hill family. The architect was R.F. Brettingham. Later additions were made, notably by the 3rd Marquess, in 1843. Originally the present drawing-room portico was the main entrance, and opened unto the Moira Road, which then ran close to the house. The present Moira Road was laid down in 1826, and the intervening parcel of ground enclosed in 1841. This explains the presence of an old Quaker burial ground within the precincts today.

Hillsborough's Main Street.

Hillsborough's Fort.

Hillsborough Georgian Doorways.

Hillsborough Main Street.

Left: Hillsborough market house.

Below: Hillsborough parish church, St Malachy's.

Hillsborough Castle.

The 6th Marquess sold the mansion and its grounds to the British government and shortly afterwards it became the official residence of the Governor of Northern Ireland. It is now the official residence of the Queen and other royal family members when visiting the province, and the Secretary of State for Northern Ireland from 1973. Hillsborough Castle was the venue for the signing of the Anglo-Irish Agreement in 1985. Former Prime Minister Tony Blair has stayed at the castle on many occasions, during negotiations related to the peace process, and hosted George W. Bush at the castle for a one-night visit in 2003.

The importance of the Downshires to the area is remembered in the prominent memorial to the **3rd Marquess of Downshire** which stands to the south of the village and is visible throughout much of the surrounding area. At the end of Main Street stands a statue of the **4th Marquess**, which was sculpted by Samuel Ferres Lynn.

The historic parish church dedicated to **St Malachy** is one of the finest examples of Gothic Revival architecture. It was built by the 1st Marquess of

Downshire between 1760 and 1774, in the hope that the church would become the Cathedral of the diocese of Down. In addition to its imposing setting, it boasts two eighteenth-century organs, a peal of ten bells and a number of works by notable craftsmen of the era, as well as the Colours of the County Down Battalion of Carson's Ulster Volunteers. Of particular interest is the governor's pew in the North Transept, on the right at the top of the steps. It is here that members of the Royal Family sit when attending Divine Worship. The composer and conductor Hamilton Harty (whose father William Harty was organist in the parish church) was born in the village in 1879.

St Malachy's, Hillsborough.

Wills Hill built the Georgian houses of the village that remain a feature to this day along with **Market House** in 1760 with the aim of attracting linen manufacturers to the area. In 1810, the north and south wings were added. The south wing of the Market House was used as an open market hall and the north wing housed a courtroom, which was operational until 1986 and now houses a display on the Irish Legal System. Hillsborough Tourist Information Centre is located in the building, which is also used for craft fairs, book fairs, art exhibitions, conferences and wedding receptions.

Heading south from Hillsborough to Newry along the A1, the town of **Dromore** is worth a visit. It is chiefly notable for its ecclesiastical history. The name is derived from *An Droim Mor*, 'the large ridge'. The town's centre is Market Square, which has a rare set of stocks. The **Cathedral Church of Christ the Redeemer** is situated on a monastic site founded by St Colman in AD 510. Dromore Cathedral is situated on the site of a medieval church, about which no record exists, and which was destroyed in the late 1500s. It was King James I who, in 1609, issued letters patent giving the church of St Colman a new title and a new status. The Cathedral church was destroyed in 1641 by Irish insurgents. A new structure, of which small portions are still visible, was built by Bishop Jeremy Taylor some twenty years later in 1661. The nucleus of today's building dates from Bishop Percy's developments in 1808, but an ancient gravestone inside the Cathedral survives and is known as 'St Colman's Pillow'.

Dromore Bailey.

Above: Dromore Town Square.

Left: The Cathedral Church of Christ the Redeemer, Dromore.

A **Celtic high cross** stands in the Cathedral grounds. The cross is made of granite and survives from the early monastery. Dromore also contains the best preserved **Anglo-Norman motte-and-bailey castle** in Ireland, which dates from the early twelfth century. It was built by Sir John de Courcy after his conquest of Down. The bailey or lower courtyard was said to have been protected by palisading and the mound itself was an archery tower, which gave good vision and a reasonable field of fire. The height and well-defined slopes provide unsurpassed views of the town and the upper Lagan Valley.

West of Hillsborough is the pretty village of **Moira** (from the Irish *Maigh Rath* meaning 'plain of ringforts'). It is a Georgian village between Lisburn and Lurgan. Nowadays, Moira is a thriving small town with an ever-growing population. In the mid-nineties Moira won numerous awards for 'Best Kept Small Town' and attracted people from miles around to see its flower displays in the Demesne and the Main Street.

Far left: Moira Castle, long since demolished.

Left and below: Moira.

In AD 637 the battle of *Mag Rath* was fought between a coalition led by Conal, King of the Dál nAraide, accompanied by Cenél nEógain of the Northern Uí Neill and Dalriada, against Domnall son of Aed of Cenél Conaill, a member of a rival branch of the Northern Uí Neill and High King of Ireland. According to the legendary cycle that sprung up around the battle, Saxons fought in alliance with Dalriada. In medieval times the district was largely owned by the O'Lavery family and their descendants. There are still 'Laverys', as they became known, living in the locality. A well-known member of this family was the distinguished painter Sir John Lavery.

Although the town existed before the seventeenth century, the Rawdon family, later Earls of Moira, were largely responsible for building the houses and for the town's development. In his estate at Moira, Sir Arthur Rawdon built the first hot-house in Europe. According to Bassett's *Directory and Guide to County Down*, published in 1886, frogs were first discovered in Ireland at Moira, probably in the magnificent botanical gardens. Sir Arthur also rebuilt the original mansion which became one of the most magnificent castles in the country. Records describe this mansion as a 'commodious habitation, surrounded by a wood, which affords beautiful walks, a large lawn extends in front, where sheep feed, and is terminated by trees, and a small Lough eastwards, the rear of the castle grounds contains a wood, with large opening fronting the castle, which forms a fine perspective'. The castle was demolished early in the nineteenth century but some of the castle's foundations can still be seen in the public park, formerly part of the grounds of Moira demesne.

In 1740, a monthly brown linen market was established in the village. By 1744, Moira was described as 'a well laid out and thriving village, consisting of one broad street, inhabited by many traders, many of whom carry on the linen trade to good advantage'. The **Market House** was built by the Bateson family, who had acquired Moira Castle in the early nineteenth century. The Market House still bears the Bateson family crest. It contained a large assembly room and a court room, which was still in use by the Courts until the early part of the nineteenth century.

A portion of ground opposite Moira Castle was given by the Hill family, later the Marquess of Downshire, for the building of the **St John's church**. The entry into the church grounds and the castle drive were in a straight line. The church was consecrated in 1723; it remains an impressive site when illuminated by lights and can be seen from the nearby MI motorway. When the church was built it had a slate steeple which was blown down in a freak storm in 1884 and was replaced by the present copper spire. The two boxes at either side of the west door were the family pews of the two principal families – the Rawdon family on the left-hand side and the Waring family on the right. The lower seating in each of these two boxes was for the respective family servants. There is reputed to have been a tunnel from Moira Castle leading to the church which was used by the Rawdon family and their servants as their means of entry. John Wesley preached in the church in 1760 and William Butler Yeats, grandfather of the famous poet of the same name was curate in 1835.

Between Moira and Lurgan and on the County Down border is the village of **Magheralin**. The origins of Magheralin are obscure, but the church has been identified with 'Lann Ronan' or the 'Church of Lan', and is mentioned in the Taxation of Pope Nicholas of 1306. The tower and transept were built during the next two centuries but the whole was in ruins in 1657. It was rebuilt after the restoration but was finally abandoned in 1845, when the new church was built across the road.

Taking an easterly direction we come to **Donaghcloney,** the 'Church of the Meadow', yet another foundation of St Patrick's. These lands were originally in the hands of the Magennis's but they were forfeited by them because of their part in the 1641 Rebellion. The lands eventually came into the ownership of William Waring, who built himself a strong mansion at Magherana around which a village grew which came to be known as Waringstown. The old parish church suffered so severely in 1641 war and later in the Williamite Wars that the private Chapel of William Waring, built in 1681 at Waringstown became the parish church. By the Victorian era, Donaghcloney had become a major centre of linen manufacture as noted in Lewis' *Topographical Dictionary* of 1837, 'There is a very extensive bleach-green at Donaghcloney, in which 8000 pieces are annually finished; and there is scarcely a house in the parish that is not, in some way, connected with this manufacture.'

A few miles south of Donaghcloney is the village of **Waringstown** which is named after William Waring, who built **Waring House** in the centre of the village in 1667. It is a three-storey gentleman's house and is the oldest unfortified mansion house in Ireland. A third-storey facade was added in 1680, designed by architect Lyndsey Boyd. In the war of 1688, William Waring was driven out by the Irish army, who kept possession of the house as a military station until the arrival of the Duke Schomberg. He remained here for two days on his march to the Boyne in July 1690. After the defeat of the Jacobite army by the Williamite forces under King William III at the Battle of the Boyne, Waring returned to Waringstown House. In spite of its eventful history, Waringstown House remains as an impressive monument to the family who did so much to development the linen industry in Ulster. The house, which is situated in the heart of the village, remains in private hands.

The Waring family brought Flemish weavers to the village, building Huguenot-style cottages for them, some of which survive today. In the past, the village was renowned for its handloom damask weaving. The industrial focus was at the southern end of the town, where brewing, linen-weaving, and cambric and clothing manufacture were formerly carried out and where some substantial eighteenth- and nineteenth-century industrial buildings still exist. In 1886, approximately 300 to 400 handloom weavers lived in the village and neighbourhood and, reputedly, it was in Waringstown that the first piece of diaper in Ireland was produced. Weaving finally ceased in 1968 with the closure of the firm of John McCollum. The village has, over the years, been associated with the sport of cricket, something that has been attributed to the area's planters being predominantly from the north of England.

In 1681, William Waring proceeded to build the church in the centre of the village, by a special Act of Parliament. It was called **Holy Trinity**, the parish church of Donaghcloney. This replaced the old church of St Patrick in Donaghcloney village. The bell of the old parish church of Donaghcloney, after having lain for many years in the River Lagan, was raised, and hung in the tower of Holy Trinity church. Engraved on it in rude characters is the inscription, 'I belong to Donaghcloney.' The church is worth a visit for the sake of its fine old timbered roof.

A few miles from Waringstown is the village of **Gilford**. The name is a contraction of 'Magill's Ford', named after Captain John Magill who acquired land in the area in the seventeenth century. The village grew up around a successful Irish linen mill and many mill houses still survive. This mill, which once employed more than 1,500 workers, closed down in 1986. It was built in the late 1830s for Hugh Dunbar who already had a thriving thread and cloth business at Huntley Glen near Banbridge. It was one of the largest flax-spinning mills in Ireland and today, although derelict, remains a sleeping giant dominating the village. In 1882 one visitor to Gilford left a fascinating account of the village in its industrial heyday:

> The manufacturing town of Gilford is a pretty, clean, neat, little place clustered round the mills and the big house, like the old feudal retainers round the castle. Here, as in Belfast, a certain amount of distress must exist, for the mills are not running full time. The wages of a common operative here is twelve shillings (or three dollars) per week. If they have a family grown up until they are able to work at the mills, of course it adds materially to the income. Girls are more precious than boys, I have heard, as being more docile and easier kept in clothing. They can earn about half wages, or six shillings (one dollar and a half) per week. Rents are about two shillings (or half a dollar) per week. It

takes one and sixpence for fuel. A young family would keep the parents busy to make ends meet in the best of times. In case of the mill running short time I should think they would persistently refuse to meet. No signs of distress, not the least were apparent any-where. The mill hands trooping past looked clean, rosy and cheerful, and were decently clad. The grounds around the factory were beautiful and very nicely kept, and beautiful also were the grounds about the great house. I felt sorry that there were no little garden plots about the tenement houses occupied by the operatives; so when hard times come they will have no potatoes or vegetables of their own to help them to tide over the times of scant wages. How I do wish that the large-hearted and generous proprietors of these works could take this matter into consideration.

From Gilford, the visitor can make their way along the A50 to **Banbridge**. Banbridge, with a population of around 18,000, is a rapidly expanding town. Its original name was Ballyvally ('The Place of the Road') and consisted of little more than a few cottages which had grown up around a bridging point on the River Bann. It was named after the first bridge built over the Upper Bann in 1712 when a new road was made from Belfast to Dublin. According to *Basset's Guide and Directory to County Down*, published in 1886, Banbridge:

> is included in the Downshire estate, and is surrounded by a good farming district. From its situation on the side of a hill, overlooking the fertile and picturesque valley of the Bann, the first view impresses a stranger most favourably; particularly if he enters by way of Laurencetown, and has an opportunity to glace in passing at the many splendid mills and bleach works lining the river banks.

The main street is very unusual in that it rises to a steep hill. Banbridge used to be an important stop on the Belfast to Dublin stagecoach route, and a number of coaching inns had been established as a result. The town's best known feature is the underpass constructed in 1834 by William Dargan, known colloquially as 'The Cut', the official name of which is 'Downshire Bridge'. It is thought that this was the first underpass ever built. Its construction was due to pressure from the Post Office, which was concerned that its horses could not pass through the centre of the town without fainting before they reached the top of the hill.

The town owes much of its early development to Wills Hill, Earl of Hillsborough who was a substantial landowner in the district. As 1st Marquess of Downshire, he laid out the town with wide streets and the market house perched on top of the hill. In 1767, he obtained a patent for holding a weekly market and five fairs annually. The town owed its success to flax and the linen industry, becoming, by

Banbridge, showing 'The Cut' *c.* 1910.

Banbridge, showing 'The Cut' today.

1772, the principal linen producing district in Ireland with a total of twenty-six bleachgreens along the Bann. The numerous falls on the river and the uniform supply of water appear to have attracted the attention of the manufacturers soon after bleaching became a separate branch of the trade.

The Market House, situated in the centre of the town, close to the viaduct, is a large and handsome edifice surmounted by a dome, and was built by the **Marquess of Downshire** in 1834. It replaced an earlier building which was demolished during the cutting of the road through the top of the hill. It is a two-storey three-bay building with a pyramidal roof topped by a square cupola with a clock-face on each side.

In the Church Square stands a striking monument to one of the most distinguished of the sons of Banbridge, **Captain Francis Rawdon Moira Crozier, R.N.** It is opposite the house where he was born in September 1796. Constructed in 1862, the monument was designed by W.J. Barre with carvings by Joseph Robinson Kirk. It carries a colossal statue of Captain Francis Crozier, and on the weathering of each of the buttresses at the base of the statue stand grieving polar bears.

Crozier was born in September 1796, the fifth son of a local solicitor. At the age of thirteen he volunteered for the Royal Navy and by 1817 had received his certificate as mate. By 1841, after several Artic expeditions, Crozier had risen to the rank of Captain and two years later was elected a Fellow of the Royal Society in recognition of his outstanding work on magnetism. Crozier was offered overall command of a further expedition in search of the north-west Passage but declined opting instead to serve as second-in-command to Sir John Franklin. They departed on 22 May 1845 and reached Greenland six weeks later. Crozier wrote to his family on 3 June and was in high spirits, 'All is prosperous; therefore all in high spirits. I like the officers very much; the first lieutenant is really a very superior fellow and the doctor – our only married man – again is a very nice proper man.'

The expedition was last spotted on 26 July but vanished shortly afterwards – their fate was to remain a mystery for many years. More than forty search parties were dispatched. One expedition, led by Dr John Richardson and Dr John Rae of the Hudson Bay Company, found a few graves of Franklin's party on Beechey Island. In 1853, Rae met a party of Esquimaux who had some belongings of the last expedition, including a silver tablespoon with Crozier's crest and the initials 'FRMC' scratched on it. He was told that four winters earlier they had met white men dragging sledges, and four months later found their bodies. Rae later established that both ships had been frozen in, between Victoria and King William islands, and the remnant of the expedition had left Beechey Island in the summer of 1846.

Scurvy had seriously depleted the crew, and when Franklin died of heart disease, Crozier had assumed command. Lady Franklin financed an expedition in 1857, under the command of Captain McClintock of Dundalk, in one last effort to discover the truth about her husband.

In May 1859, a sledge party discovered under a cairn in the extreme north-west of King William Island, a document dated 25 April 1848. The document ended, 'Sir John Franklin died on the 11 June, 1847, and the total loss by deaths in the expedition has been to this date nine officers, and fifteen men. FRM Crozier, captain and senior officer. Start on tomorrow for the Backs Fish River.' Rae discovered that some reached this river on the mainland, but all had finally died. Much to the horror of Victorian Britain, the men had resorted to cannibalism in the end.

The search for the truth about the fate of Crozier and his colleagues continues to this day. In 1985, the graves from Franklin's first winter camp were opened, revealing three remarkably well-preserved bodies, looking not much different from the way they did when first buried.

One, John Torrington, had his eyes open and was remarkably well-preserved for a man who had spent nearly 140 years buried in the ice. Scientists took the opportunity to measure the lead levels in the soft tissue and hair from these bodies, as well as from bones recovered from King William Island, and found that at least some of the Franklin crew-members had suffered from lead poisoning, brought about by their canned foods.

There are no less than eight separate points in the world named after Francis Crozier, acknowledging his contribution towards exploration and science. These include three Cape Croziers, Crozier Strait which lies between Cornwallis and Bathurst Islands, and the Crozier River which is found near Fury and Hecla Strait.

Banbridge is in the parish of Seapatrick, and the ruins of the old church may still be seen in a graveyard about a mile away. This very ancient ecclesiastical site is said to have been founded by St Patrick who, legend has it, crossed the River Bann at Ballykeel Ford to give his horse a drink. There was a church on the site in 1306 and one was destroyed in 1641. The ruined building, now standing, was built in 1698 and abandoned in 1837 after the present **Seapatrick parish church** was built in the town of Banbridge in 1834. What was probably a holy well is remembered in a little memorial beside the old graveyard.

The quiet river valley running between Banbridge and Rathfriland is referred to as the **Brontë Homeland**. The reason for this apparently strange reference to a family more readily associated with Yorkshire, is because Emdale, County Down is the childhood home of Patrick Brontë, father of the three famous literary sisters, Charlotte, Emily, and Anne. The ruins of his cottage at Emdale are still preserved

Scarvagh House.

and in the care of the Brontë Homeland trust since 1956. Patrick Brontë lived and worked in this area before moving to Haworth in Yorkshire.

The Brontë Homeland Drive starts at Drumballyroney church and school near Rathfriland, ten miles south of Banbridge. It is well signposted along the ten-mile route. Together Drumballyroney church and school are known as the **Brontë Interpretive Centre**. **Alice McClory's Cottage** was the childhood home of Patrick's mother, Alice McClory. **Glascar School** (Glascar Road) was where Patrick taught in the 1790s, although the original schoolhouse was replaced by a more modern building in 1844.

A short distance from Banbridge is the historic village of **Loughbrickland** situated on the lake from which it takes its name, which was well known before Banbridge rose to prominence. The village was founded by Sir Marmaduke Whitechurch around 1585 for English Protestant settlers. Local tradition refers to an early monastic foundation, a Franciscan house which is believed to have prospered in the townland of Drumsallagh from the early fifteenth century until 1569, when it suffered suppression under Elizabeth I. The monastery may have been quarried to provide building materials for the original Church of Ireland church in Loughbrickland, constructed in 1600. In June 1690, William III camped near Loughbrickland with his army on his march to the Boyne.

Whyte's Estate Historical Trial takes the visitor through woodland and country lanes and contains two scheduled historic monumentts: Coolnacran Fort, a rath on the eastern side of a drumlin, and Johnston's Fort a raised rath which offers a great view down to Loughbrickland Village.

The village of **Scarva** (from the Irish *Scarbhach* meaning 'shallow ford') is also closely associated with William III. Scarva stands on the very western boundary of County Down and on the main road west of Banbridge. It is closely identified with the Newry Canal which operated for over 200 years and provided employment for local people. However, the growth of the railway industry had disastrous consequences for the canal and eventually led to its closure in 1947. The listed curving terrace of houses in Main Street are small in scale and face what was originally a small dock on the Newry Canal. The gradual curve of the street ends in the Presbyterian church and graveyard to the south.

In June 1690, an army of 30,000 men camped in the Scarva area for training before marching on to meet the forces of King James at the Battle of the Boyne on 12 July 1690. Whilst training his army, King William is said to have camped under a magnificent Spanish chestnut tree which still flourishes. Each year, a **Sham Fight** takes place on the 13 July on the old training ground used, which is now part of the demense of Scarvagh House. The house was built in 1527 with further improvements added over a 200-year period. Today it is one of the Ulster's premier horse-breeding establishments.

At **Scarva Visitor Centre**, located in the village, visitors can trace the history of canal building and the role of the Newry Canal in the linen industry. Interpretative boards within the centre help to explain the building of the Canal, its trade and Scarva's role within this.

Chapter 7

The Kingdom of Mourne

Sing a song of pleasant beaches
Where the mountains meet the sea.
Sing of woods and shadowed streamlets
From the uplands bounding free.
Sing of crags against the high sky,
Shepherd's path and quarry track,
Stone fringed fields, scots pine and fuchsia,
All the things that call us back.

Song of the Mournes
From 'Wayfarer in the Mournes' By J.S. Doran

The Mourne Mountains, made famous through Percy French's song 'Where the Mountains of Mourne sweep down to the sea', remain, for many people, their most vivid memory of a visit to County Down. H.V. Morton thought the Mournes 'some of the most beautiful mountains in all Ireland'. In his opinion:

> They are different from the blue hills of Donegal, different from the weird peaks of Kerry or the wild highlands of the West; yet they are linked to all these by that unearthly quality of the Irish landscape which I can describe only as something which seems half in this world and half in the next.

Author C.S. Lewis admitted that the varied landscapes of the Mournes inspired some of his fabulous Chronicles of Narnia. Visitors today can still enjoy the magic that inspired C.S. Lewis if they take one of the many beautiful walks which transverse these magnificent mountain ranges.

Slieve Donard Hotel.

The Mourne Mountains were formed 65 million years ago, and are made of granite, which is an igneous rock. Many of the mountains have names beginning with *Slieve*, from the Irish word *sliabh*, meaning, appropriately enough, 'mountain'. There are twelve peaks over 2,000 feet high, including Northern Ireland's highest mountain, Slieve Donard. The Mournes are unusual in that their summits are grouped together in a compact area, only seven miles in breadth and fourteen miles long, forming a crescent across the map. They run down to the sea for only a brief stretch between Newcastle and Annalong, and again along a much lower ridge at Rostrevor, on Carlingford Lough.

Northern Ireland's highest mountain, **Slieve Donard** is named after St Domangart, or Domangard, also known as St Donard who was a follower of St Patrick. St Donard, who died in around 506, lived inside a stone cell on top of the mountain now named after him. The many legends told about St Donard illustrate the heroic efforts he made to convert his countrymen. He later established his monastery at Maghera, probably inside the rath where a ruined church of medieval date still stands.

On the top of Slieve Donard there are two cairns, one on the very summit and the other, called the 'Lesser Cairn' on the Ordnance Survey maps, some 800 feet to the north-east. Both of these have been much disturbed. The Summit Cairn has been tampered with by sappers and water commissioners and the Lesser Cairn has small piles of stones about it, but it is difficult to say whether these are ancient structures or just re-arrangements by modern hands.

The view from the top of Donard is spectacular. Look north, and all County Down lies beneath you. You can see Downpatrick lying on its wooded hill, and beyond is the glorious fretted outline of Strangford Lough dotted with its green islands. Look north-west and you will see the broad silver sea that is Lough Neagh, and east of this are the Belfast Hills. Westward are miles of brown mountains and in the south you can see the cone-shaped hills that lie south of Dublin in County Wicklow, eighty miles away. Looking eastward over the Irish Sea you see is Dundrum Bay and far off is the Isle of Man lying half way between Ireland and England, the base of so many Viking raids on the County Down coast.

In the 1890s the water commissioners, to service a growing population in Belfast and County Down with water, decided to enclose a reservoir's catchment area in the Mourne Mountains with a wall, which stretches twenty-two miles over eleven peaks. It was started in 1904 and, with a break in the war years, was completed in 1922. Work started in March and ended in mid-October each year and provided much-needed employment in the area. The wall rises and falls over fifteen mountains including Slieve Donard, Slieve Commedagh, and Slieve Binnian. Today it is popular with hikers, providing views unsurpassed in Northern Ireland.

The Mournes have many attractions for hikers, and many of the most popular walks are closely associated with local folklore. An impressive chasm, called **Maggie's Leap**, is named after a pretty young girl who was collecting seagull eggs along the rocks when she became startled by an unwelcome suitor. In her haste to be rid of him she leapt over the chasm and landed safely on the other side without breaking a single egg in her basket. Near Maggie's Leap is the **Bloody Bridge**, which was originally a ford. The name refers to a massacre at the site at the time of the 1641 Rebellion. The bodies of slain prisoners were thrown over the bridge into the river, turning it red and so the river became known as the Bloody Bridge River. A few centuries ago, sought-after commodities such as brandy, wine, silk, tobacco, and tea were smuggled ashore and transported along the **Brandy Path** to Hilltown and surrounds. Following the path of the smugglers demonstrates that you don't have to climb to a summit to appreciate the beauty of the Mourne Mountains. Perhaps for this reason many people believe it to be one of the best walks in the Mournes.

The ancient Kingdom of Mourne, although never a kingdom in the true sense of the word, somehow, in its rural grandeur, deserves the name. The coastal plain of Mourne was settled by Stone Age people whose cairns and dolmens are still to be seen. Viking raids began in the ninth century, giving Carlingford Lough (Carlinn Fjord) its name, as they used it as a route to Newry and further inland in search of pillage. Annalong (in Irish *Alt na Long*, 'the ford of the ships') also recalls their influence.

Throughout the Middle Ages, the Mournes were a borderland between the thin coastal strip held by the Anglo-Normans and the Irish-held interior. Mourne came under Norman influence in the thirteenth century, when castles at Carlingford,

Greencastle, and Dundrum were built by John de Courcy. Until the early 1800s, the area's only connection with the outside world was by sea, and along the coast to Newcastle and Newry. Even with the construction of a third highway through the mountains, the coastal lowlands remained a place apart until comparatively recently.

For many visitors to the Mournes, the picturesque seaside resort of **Newcastle** is the most popular place to stop and appreciate the beauty of the surrounding countryside. The town has gone through a major rejuvenation in recent times with its new promenade winning a number of national awards. Newcastle is an ideal base to explore the Mourne Mountains, which tower spectacularly over the town.

The town derives its name from a castle erected by a chieftain of the clan McGinnis near the mouth of the Shimna River towards the end of the fifteenth century. The castle has long since disappeared, the remains being finally demolished by the Earl Annesley who built a hotel in the nineteenth century.

Newcastle became a popular resort during the nineteenth century, being dubbed 'the queen of Northern bathing-places' by Dr Alexander Know in his book *The Irish Watering Places*, published in 1845. According to McComb's *Guide to Belfast*, published in 1861:

> Newcastle is very neatly built, and every year handsome buildings for the accommodation of sea-bathers are being added. The beach is a hard sandy bottom, and the sea-water is clear and pure, and suited in graduation of depth to the capacities and tastes of all classes of bathers. The village is well sheltered, by the mountain barrier in the rear, from the South-Westerly winds, which prevail about eight months in the year. These recommendations, in conjunction with the varied and enchanting scenery of the vicinity, have rendered Newcastle the most aristocratic and generally-patronised watering-place on the Down coast.

Above left: Annalong Corn Mill.

Above right: Newcastle in the 1930s.

In the 1820s, Lord Annesley created a new pier here, to function primarily as a loading point for the famous Mourne granite, which was extracted from the overlooking hills. Blocks of this granite were used to build docks in Belfast and Liverpool, as well as help construct the Albert memorial in London. Today the harbour still holds some fishing boats and also has pleasure crafts for water sports.

The sea has also provided Newcastle with its share of tragedies. Most famously, on 13 January 1843, boats from Newcastle and Lower Mourne set out for the usual fishing stations, and were caught in a gale. Seventy-six men perished, forty-six of whom were from Newcastle. They left twenty-seven widows, one hundred and eighteen children, and twenty-one dependants. A Public Subscription was raised and the cottages, known as **Widows' Row**, were built for the widows and dependants close to the harbour. A local song about the disaster says 'Newcastle town is one long street entirely stripped of men.'

Newcastle's popularity was further boosted by the arrival of the railway in 1869. Sadly the impressive station closed in May 1955 and it now used as a supermarket. In 1910, **Harry Ferguson** flew a small plane across Newcastle beach in one of the first engine powered flights by aircraft in Ireland. He completed the flight in an attempt to win a £100 prize, offered by the town, for the first powered flight along the strand. His first take off ended badly, but according to a modern newspaper report, 'He flew a distance of almost three miles along the foreshore at a low altitude varying between fifty and five hundred feet.' This event is recorded by a plaque on the promenade. The promenade also features a metal sculpture that depicts a perforated outline of **Percy French**, surrounded by the words of his 'Mountains of Mourne' song which, since its publication in 1896, has done so much to promote the area around the world.

Donard Park, behind the town, tends to be overshadowed by the proximity of the forest park of Tollymore, but it has fine walks from the car park up the tumbling Glen River. The **Slieve Donard Hotel** is perhaps Newcastle's most impressive building. The hotel stands in six acres of private grounds which lead to the world famous Royal County Down Golf Club. It was built by the Belfast and County Down Railway, as an 'end of line' luxury holiday destination. Construction started in 1896, and was completed and officially opened on 24 June 1898 at a cost of £44,000. Former guests at the hotel include have included Percy French, Charlie Chaplin, and King Leopold.

The **Murlough Nature Reserve** is situated between Dundrum and Newcastle off the A2 and is well worth a visit. It is a fragile 6,000-year-old sand dune system, owned by the National Trust and managed as Ireland's first nature reserve since 1967. It is an excellent area for walking and bird watching due to its spectacular location at the edge of Dundrum Bay and the Mourne Mountains.

A few miles north from Newcastle along the A2 is **Dundrum** (from the Irish *Dún Droma* meaning 'fort on the ridge'). Dundrum is situated on the western shore of Dundrum Inner Bay, a shallow sandy tidal area, connected to the open sea by a narrow channel. It was an important port until 1984. Coal, in particular, was a major import into Dundrum, where the East Downshire Steamship Company was based. The beautiful bay has had a dangerous reputation for mariners for centuries because of the prevalence of south and south-easterly winds, and the strong tidal current from north and south which meet at this part of the shore. Many shipwrecks have found themselves in the bay, including that of the SS *Great Britain*. Designed by Isambard Kingdom Brunel, the SS *Great Britain* was on its way from Liverpool to New York in 1846 when it ran aground during bad weather in Dundrum Bay. The captain, James Hosken, miscalculated the steamer's speed, and with poor charts, was responsible for a series of 'truly inexplicable' navigational errors which resulted in the ship running aground in Dundrum Bay. It took a year to re-float the ship but it continued to be in use for many years before being installed as a visitor attraction in Bristol, where it can still be seen.

No trip to **Dundrum** is complete without a visit to **Dundrum Castle**. Built to control access into Lecale from the west and south, it stands on the top of a rocky hill above the village. The earliest fortification was a motte-and-bailey built by John de Courcy in the late 1170s. In 1204, de Courcy was expelled from Ulster by Hugh de Lacy who strengthened the castle with a massive round keep, probably employing master masons from the Welsh Marches, where such keeps were then popular. The castle was captured by King John in 1210 and remained Crown property until de Lacy was allowed to return to his Earldom in 1226. The Magennis family of Mourne seized Dundrum in the late 1400s and, with a few intervals, held the castle until it was surrendered to Lord Mountjoy in 1601. The Magennis family recaptured Dundrum in 1642, but later lost it to the Parliamentarians, who disabled the castle as a military base in 1652, after they withdrew their garrison. It remains, nevertheless, an impressive site perched on the hillside above Dundrum and offers fabulous views south over Dundrum Bay and the Mourne Mountains.

North-west from Newcastle along the A50 the town of **Castlewellan** has a wide main street which runs through two main squares lined with chestnut trees. In the sixteenth century, Castlewellan was a stronghold and one of the chief seats of the Magennis family. Under James I it was forfeited to the Crown, but later Phelim Magennis was granted eleven townlands in the parishes of Kilmegan and Kilcoo, constituting the Manor of Castlewellan. The lands at Castlewellan passed

Above left: Harry Ferguson.

Above right: Dundrum Castle 1791

Left: Dundrum Castle today.

into the possession of the Annesley family in 1742 when they were purchased from Arthur Magennis, though the family had previously resided there for some years on lease. Mrs Delany, wife of the Dean of Down, a tenant of the Annesleys' at Dundrum, wrote to her sister informing her that the Annesleys had 'walled in and planted with oak, etc., 350 acres of ground for a park. Near them is a large bleach yard, and Mr Annesley is going to build a town.' The town was designed by a French architect for the Annesley family and is unique within Ireland due to its tree-lined squares, both in the old town (upper square) and new town (lower square) as well as its very wide main street. The old **Market House** in the upper square was built in 1764 and now houses the public library. The Scottish baronial style **Castlewellan Castle**, now a conference centre, was formerly the house of the Annesley family. The castle was constructed in 1751, from local granite and overlooks a mile-long lake surrounded by woodland and mature parkland. The estate now forms **Castlewellan Forest Park**, with its magnificent lake and the arboretum which was begun in 1740 and contains plants and trees from many different countries including Spain, Mexico and Wales. The Peace Maze, the world's largest permanent hedge maze according to Guinness World Records, was constructed in the park between 2000 and 2001.

Between Newcastle and Castlewellan, on the Byransford Road is **Tolymore Forest Park** which was previously owned by Robert Jocelyn, 8th Earl of Roden and purchased by the Department of Agriculture in 1930 and 1941. It was Northern Ireland's first forest park when it opened in 1955. The Roden mansion has been demolished but the demesne is celebrated for its follies, gateways and bridges. Covering an area of almost 630 hectares at the foot of the Mourne Mountains, the forest park offers panoramic views of the surrounding mountains and the sea at nearby Newcastle, while within its own boundaries a walk along the Shimna River includes rocky outcrops, bridges, grottos, and caves. The main entrance, the Barbican Gate, has castellated turrets and quatrefoil loopholes, and the Bryansford Gate (the exit) has a Gothic arch, pinnacles and flying buttresses.

Another detour on the B180 road between Newcastle and Castlewellan is the ancient foundation of **Maghera**. Since its foundation in the sixth century, this monastic site has been associated with St Donard (Domongart), after whom Slieve Donard, the highest peak in the Mournes, has been named. The ruins of the medieval church and burial ground surrounded by an ancient rath remain. There are two pre-Norman cross-craved stones and a thirteenth-century coffin lid used as a headstone in the graveyard. Nearby are the remnants of Maghera round tower. Built in about the early tenth century, this once impressive structure was blown down in a storm in the early eighteenth century.

South from Newcastle is the town of **Kilkeel**, the 'capital of the Mournes', which takes its name from the old church overlooking the town, it being the anglicised version of the Gaelic *Cill Chaoil* meaning 'narrow church' or 'The church of/in the narrow place.' The name may be drawn from **Kilkeel old church** and graveyard which is situated to the west of Newcastle Street and north of Bridge Street. Within the ground of the church there is a defaced equal-armed medieval cross which stands beside a well, popularly believed to cure warts. The church was constructed in 1388 and dedicated to 'St Colman Del Mourne' while the graveyard attached to the church was used for burials until 1916, long after the church had been abandoned.

Local legend has it that William Hare, one of the notorious killers who terrorised Edinburgh in the 1820s, died and was buried in Kilkeel. His accomplice, William Burke, was hanged for the murders, while Hare was granted immunity from prosecution. Hare was released in February 1829, and many popular tales tell of him as a blind beggar on the streets of London where he died destitute. However, none of these reports were ever confirmed. It is certainly possible, given the harsh Poor Law system in operation from the late 1830s, that Hare was forced to return to his place of origin before he would be admitted to the workhouse.

Maghera church.

Fishing is a major industry in Kilkeel, with Kilkeel Harbour the home port for the largest fishing fleet in Northern Ireland. There are fish-processing factories around the port, pleasure angling off the piers and lobster farming along the coastline. The **Nautilus Centre** which overlooks the port is a good place to enjoy scenery while enjoying a meal in the first-floor restaurant. The main focal point of the building is the Heritage Centre which takes up part of the shop. There is a multimedia system which, at the touch of the computer screen, will tell you everything you could ever wish to know about fishing in Kilkeel port.

Near Kilkeel are two interesting earthen forts or 'duns', at **Dunavan** and **Dunavil**. To the east of the town is a fine cromleac that is known locally as the **Crawtree Stone**. In a field beside the Catholic cemetery at **Massforth** is a good example of a 'giant's grave' (Kistvaen). The covering stones are missing, but the upright ones are still intact. Five miles from Kilkeel is **Greencastle** which was, for centuries, the capital of the Kingdom of Mourne and later an important stronghold of the Anglo-Norman power in Ulster. The castle was built by Hugh de Lacy, almost certainly during the 1230s, to protect the southern approaches to the Earldom of Ulster. It has been attacked and destroyed numerous times by Irish armies, Scots under Edward Bruce, and Parliamentary forces in 1652. The design of Hugh de Lacy's castle consisted of a quadrilateral curtain wall with a D-shaped tower at each corner – all now in a very fragmentary state. For centuries the green below the castle played host to a great fair every August. It was often called 'Ram Fair' as a great ram was customarily enthroned on top of the castle's walls.

Further along the coast is **Cranfield Bay**, with a fine bathing strand. Cranfield beach is a Blue Flag Beach and is set in an idyllic location at the mouth of Carlingford Lough with the Mourne Mountains as a backdrop. The long south-facing beach offers excellent facilities for all visitors, whether it is for a gentle stroll or for water-based activities.

Kilkeel is about four miles from the important **Silent Valley Reservoir**, which supplies most of the water to Northern Ireland. With Belfast's rapid growth, there was a fast-growing demand for more and more water. Between 1947 and 1951, over 150 men drove a tunnel almost two and a half miles long underneath Slieve Binnian. The tunnel was built to carry water from the Annalong valley to the Silent Valley Dam, which had been completed in 1933, fourteen years earlier. Two work squads began at each end of the tunnel led by candle light. When the two squads met, they were mere inches off.

The Silent Valley is an area of Outstanding Natural Beauty. The park is surrounded with breathtaking countryside, to the east Craggy Binnian, to the west the Cliffs of Slievenag Lough, and to the north Doon and Ben Crom. The information centre and café are housed in two old colonia-style bungalows, the last remnants of the construction period. The information centre tells the story of the Silent Valley via the exhibition.

One of the most beautiful routes into the Mourne Mountains is that from Banbridge over the mountains through Rathfriland and Hilltown and on to Tolymore Forest Park. **Rathfriland** ('Frielan's Fort'), on a lofty hill, about three miles from Hilltown, is an interesting old town with its water tower visible for miles. This was, for a long period, a seat of the petty chiefs of Iveagh, whose descendant Art Magennis, 1st Viscount Iveagh built a castle around 1611.

The large town square was the site of a thriving market for many years which, like the town, has now fallen into decline. The Market House, which stands in the centre, was built in 1764 and stands where there was formerly a village pond. The ruins of an old castle may still be seen on the hill, upon which the town is situated. The stone was quarried from the hill itself, and created a steep precipice on the west side which would have been useful in defending the site. The steepness of the site can still be appreciated, when approaching the town from the Banbridge direction. Following the defeat of the 1641 Rebellion, the castle was destroyed by Cromwell's General Ireton and the manor of Rathfriland was granted to Alderman William Hawkins. His son, John Hawkins, finally pulled down most of the castle and built a new manor house in the townland of Lessize below the town. In his *County Down Guide and Directory*, published in 1886, George Henry Bassett described the site of the old castle:

> The streets of the town, all consisting of good substantial slated houses, run up and down, and across the hill. At the summit are three walls of the castle, the highest being about 26 feet, and having a breadth of 27 feet. They are in the garden of Mr. James Nelson, who comfortable dwelling stands at a distance of about 40 feet. It was built in 1812 by the

Far left:
Rathfriland.

Left:
Rathfriland
Market House.

Scott family, and during the excavation for the foundations several dungeons were found. Human bones, coins and pieces of armour were turned up at the same time.

All that remains standing today of Rathfriland Castle is a small portion of the south gable wall measuring 30 feet long by 25 feet wide. When it was finally taken down by John Hawkins, the stones were said to have been used to build some of the oldest buildings of the town. Among those which have survived is the old three-storey 'Town Inn' which still stands at the corner of The Square and Newry Street. The cellar of this building was said to be the meeting place of the notorious 'Hellfire Club' in the eighteenth century.

A few miles from Rathfriland is **Hilltown**, a small angling village, located at a crossroads on top of a hill. It was named after Lord Hill, later the Marquess of Downshire, the founder of Hilltown and Hillsborough. The Hills founded the village in 1766 so that people living in the area could find employment in the linen industry. Hilltown has eight public houses in the high street, a legacy from eighteenth-century smugglers who shared out their contraband here. The River Bann at Hilltown is a well-known trout river and has attracted anglers for generations.

Leaving Hilltown, the visitor should head along the B27 Kilkeel Road which takes you over the Mourne Mountains to Tolymore Forest Park and Newcastle. It is one of the most beautiful drives in Northern Ireland, as you make your way to **Spelga Dam** and Reservoir, which sits amongst the Mourne Mountains at over 1,200 feet above sea level. The Spelga Reservoir itself was developed between 1953 and 1957 and supplies the Portadown and Banbridge areas with water. The Spelga Pass descends from the Deer's Meadow and along the headwater of the River Bann to the Hilltown lowlands. In the eighteenth and early nineteenth centuries, farmers and their families grazed cattle on the lush upland pastures over the summer months and remnants of their temporary 'booleys' (summer huts), can still be found east of Spelga Dam. This practice has long since ceased, but is recalled in Slievenamiskan (Butter-tub Mountain) and Butter Mountain.

Chapter 8

Newry

The cathedral city of Newry is, for many people, the gateway to the magnificent countryside of south Down, standing as it does at the head of Carlingford Lough. Although partly in County Armagh it is historically more associated with County Down. The River Clanrye, which runs through the city, forms the historic border between the two counties. The cross-border rail link between Northern Ireland and the Republic serves Newry, which enjoys a frequent express service to Belfast and Dublin in addition to local services. Robin Bryans, writing in the early 1960s, summed up the charm of Newry:

> There were some factories on the outskirts and some warehouses in the town, but not enough to ruin the place as industry inevitably does. Newry, in fact, had escaped comparatively unscathed from the nineteenth century, and looked very much as it must have done from the seventeenth century onwards. In character, the town shared much of the regularity and the idea of straight streets common to most Ulster towns. But Newry also had an alien and pleasing quality, approximating to the Dutch flavour found in Fenland towns in England.

Although an ancient settlement, Newry only became a city in 2002. The city sits in a valley, nestled between the Mourne Mountains to the east, and the Ring of Gullion to the south-west, both of which are designated Areas of Outstanding Natural Beauty. Because of its strategic position, the town was repeatedly destroyed in the wars for the control of Ulster. Newry is named after a yew tree said to have been planted by St Patrick. According to legend, St Patrick planted the yew tree at the head of the strand of Carlingford Lough, where it flourished for the best part of seven centuries. The town took its name from this story, with the old name being *Iuir Cinn Tra* (Yew at the Strand's Head), which eventually was revised and shortened to the word Newry.

A Cistercian Abbey was founded in 1157 by Murtagh McLoughlin, King of Ireland and a settlement grew up alongside the abbey. The abbey was burnt in 1162, along with the yew tree as the *Annals of the Four Masters* relate, 'the monastery of the Monks at Iubhar Chinntrochta was burned, with all its furniture and books, and also the Yew Tree which Patrick himself had planted'. A later story states that an offshoot of the yew tree was planted and flourished. This tree survived until the town's destruction in the seventeenth century, and probably provides the second yew on the arms of Newry. The abbey and its lands were later granted to Nicholas Bagena by Edward VI in 1550 who adopted the Abbot's house as a residence for himself. According to *Bradshaw's General Directory*, published in 1820, part of the building still remained and was occupied as two dwelling houses:

> The walls are extremely thick and strong; and the alterations in the building which have been made in modern times were attended with unusual difficulty and labour. Within the last sixty years, there was a very massive stone stair-case outside the building. It was no easy task to take this down, owing to the extreme hardness and solidity of the work. It is said that the men employed found it necessary to blow it up with gunpowder.

Newry became an important centre again under Anglo-Norman rule, during the later part of the twelfth century. The Normans established two castles in Newry. The first was down by the river, where it could guard the bridge. It was later burnt by Edward Bruce in 1315. After being rebuilt, it was again destroyed by the O'Neills. The second was five or six miles further along the Clanrye River which survives as the Crown Mound in the townland of Sheeptown.

The re-establishment of Crown authority over the Newry area was carried out by Nicholas Bagenal who was tasked with 'the reduction of those rude and savage quarters to better rule and obedience.' Bagenal was a colourful figure and appears to have come to Ireland after being implicated in a murder. After serving for a period of time as a mercenary soldier for the O'Neills, he received a general pardon in 1543. This pardon has led some historians to believe that Bagenal may have been acting as a double agent on behalf of the Crown. In 1547, he was appointed Marshall of Elizabeth's army in Ireland and, in 1550, was given a lease 'of the college or house of Newry'. In many ways Bagenel was the real founder of the town of Newry. He colonised it, rebuilt the castle, and in 1578, erected the parish church of St Patrick's, perhaps the earliest Protestant church in Ireland.

During the Williamite Wars, (1689-1691) Newry was destroyed by fire. In an effort to deprive the enemy of food and shelter, the Jacobite forces put the town to the torch. Early in the eighteenth century, the Earl of Hillsborough planned a new town. This was located on the lower ground adjacent to the river. Hill Street (named after the Earl), formed the central spine of the new town. The new streets were broader and the houses more elegant than they had been. This is the town as we know it today.

By the middle of the eighteenth century, Newry was a bustling and significant town. Low-lying marshland along the river and canal was drained and reclaimed. Housing and businesses were built, and the town expanded to Ballybot on the Armagh side of the river. By 1770, Newry possessed 1,600 houses, many of elegant style and decoration, and the town had its own theatre. Industry flourished around the canal, linen mills, breweries, saltworks, a sugar refinery, and an iron foundry. Newry grew to become an international trading centre, trading with America, Jamaica, the Baltics, Poland, France, and England. The commercial growth of the town increased its political influence.

In 1742, the composer George Frederick Handel came to Newry to perform his work *Alexander's Feast*. Jonathan Swift was a frequent visitor as he travelled on his way to Loughry House and Gosford, and is remembered for his couplet that describes Newry at this time:

High Church, Low steeple,
Dirty Streets and Proud people

Newry in its heyday was very much a canal town and it is the canal, completed in 1742, that was a major impetus for industrial growth in many of County Armagh's towns, including Tandragee and Portadown, until the arrival of the railways a century later. Sadly derelict now, when it was a bustling thoroughfare it connected the city with the fertile agricultural land and busy mills of County Armagh all the way to Lough Neagh. The canal had a total length of 18½ miles with thirteen locks including those at Poyntzpass, Whitecoat Point where it joined up with the River Bann, Portadown and finally Lough Neagh. Newry prospered, after the opening of the canal, and by 1777 was the fourth largest port in Ireland and the largest in the north of Ireland creating many wealthy merchants.

The town's mercantile past is reflected in names such as Buttercrane Quay, Sugar Island and Sugarhouse Quay. The main export was linen, Tyrone coal, Mourne granite, and farm produce. For those with a little time to spare, and who fancy a little exercise, the **Newry Towpath route**, which stretches from Newry Town Hall to the Bann Bridge at Portadown, a distance of twenty miles, is a great way to appreciate the unique beauty and industrial and archaeological history of County Down and Armagh.

By the early nineteenth century Newry had become a major commercial centre. Lewis points out in his *Topographical Dictionary*, published in 1837:

Newry is much more a commercial than a manufacturing town. There are two iron-foundries, each on an extensive scale, for light castings. The manufacture of flint glass is also carried on largely; a distillery in Monaghan-street consumes annually 25,000 barrels of grain, the produce of which is consumed in the counties of Down, Armagh, Louth, and Monaghan: there are also large manufactories of cordage and of spades, shovels, and other kinds of ironmongery. One of the most complete and extensive bleach-greens in the country is at Carnmeen; and at Bessbrook is a mill for spinning linen yarn. The Newry flour-mills, worked by water, consume 900 tons of wheat annually, and there are several others in the immediate neighbourhood, the produce of which is mostly shipped to Liverpool. An oatmeal-mill grinds 17,000 barrels of grain annually, which is wholly purchased for the Liverpool and Manchester markets; and in the neighbour-hood there ate several others equally extensive.

Newry Town Hall.

William Makepeace Thackeray, who visited Newry during its Victorian heyday was equally impressed by Newry, declaring that the town was:

> ... remarkable as being the only town I have seen which had no cabin suburb: strange to say, the houses begin all at once, handsomely coated and hatted with stone and slate; and if Dundalk was prosperous, Newry is better still. Such a sight of neatness and comfort is exceedingly welcome to an English traveller, who, moreover, finds himself, after driving through a plain bustling clean street, landed at a large plain comfortable inn, where business seems to be done, where there are smart waiters to receive him, and a comfortable warm coffee room that bears no traces of dilapidation.

He was found the town prosperous and thriving:

> Newry has many comfortable and handsome public buildings: the streets have a business-like look, the shops and people are not too poor, and the southern grandiloquence is not shown here in the shape of fine words for small wares. Even the beggars are not so numerous, I fancy, or so coaxing and wheedling in their talk. Perhaps, too, among the gentry, the same moral change may be remarked, and they seem more downright and plain in their manner; but one must not pretend to speak of national characteristics from such a small experience as a couple of evenings' intercourse may give.

The railways arrived in 1849, leading to the sharp decline in the fortunes of the canal and with that Newry's importance decreased as Belfast's dominance in Ulster grew. By 1881, the population of Newry had reached its nineteenth-century zenith of 15,590 but from the turn of the century until the 1960s there was a period of decline as the inland canal, the mills, factories, and tramways all closed. The Troubles during the closing decades of the twentieth century further undermined Newry, but the city emerged in the new century with renewed vigour. These days Newry is one of the country's foremost commercial centres; extensive shopping and entertainment complexes include the Quays and Buttercrane Centres.

Newry has the unique distinction of being the only city in Ireland without a Church of Ireland Cathedral. **Saint Patrick's church**, built in 1578 on the instructions of Nicholas Bagenal, is considered to be the first Protestant church in Ireland. The church was, however, rebuilt in its current form in 1866. It is a roughcast, granite building with rectangular windows in the church and Gothic windows in the tower. The church sits on a hill on Church Street on the east side of the city and occupies a commanding position overlooking the city centre. It is notable for its unusual spire, consisting of a small steeple at each corner of the clock tower.

Late Victorian Newry.

Newry town centre, today.

Above left: St Patrick's church, Newry

Above right: Bagenal's Castle.

Down the hill is **Hill Street**, one of Newry's oldest streets, which appears on a map of the town dating from 1568. At the foot of High Street is **St Clare's Convent**. Turing left into **Castle Street** is the Victoria Bakery and **Bagenal's Castle**. The Victoria Bakery stands on the site of the old Cistercian Abbey which was founded in 1144. According to surviving records, Nicholas Bagenal lived in Abbot's House in the 1550s before building a castle. This site became the location of McCann's Bakery in 1837 and it was not until the bakery closed in 1997, that the original sixteenth-century structure of the castle was found to have survived inside the bakery buildings. These buildings are now the venue for **Newry and Mourne Museum** which was established in 1986. Its diverse collections currently include material relating to prehistory; Newry's Cistercian foundations; Ulster's Gaelic Order and its relationship with the English Crown; the building of a merchant town and the first summit level canal in the British Isles; the working life and folk traditions of rural and mountain areas; fishing, trade and migration by sea; renowned local personalities and businesses; folklore, storytelling and music, and modern experiences of a Border area. All these aspects of local heritage are explored at through a varied programme of exhibitions, educational events and activities.

Across the busy road from the museum is the imposing edifice the Tudor-Gothic **Cathedral of St Patrick and St Colman**, which is undoubtedly the most commanding building in the town centre, and is arguably the most important work executed by Newry's greatest native architect Thomas Duff. Built in 1829, of local granite to a cost of £8,000, it was the first Catholic Cathedral opened after the granting of Catholic Emancipation in 1829. The tower and transept were added in 1888 whilst in 1904 the nave was extended. The interior marble work and mosaics took five years to complete, with craftsmen coming from Italy to undertake the work.

Rear view St Patrick's and St Colman's RC Cathedral.

Close to the Cathedral is **St Michel Place and St Colman's Park** which is home to the statue which was erected in memory of **John Mitchel** (1815-1875) who, more than any other writer or politician, shaped the nationalist perception of the Great Famine. Born in Londonderry, his father was appointed minister of Newry Presbyterian church in 1823, and the family moved to Dromalane House. Mitchel was educated at Dr Henderson's classical school at Newry before graduating from Trinity College, Dublin, in 1834. After an attempt at working as a bank clerk, he entered the office of John Henry Quinn, a solicitor at Newry. At the close of 1836, he eloped with Jane Verner, a sixteen-year-old schoolgirl. The fugitives were captured at Chester, and Mitchel was taken back in custody to Ireland, where he was kept a few days in prison before being released on bail. Their second attempt was, however, more successful, and on 3 February 1837 they were married at Drumcree church. The marriage was said to have been extremely happy, and the couple had six children.

Left and below left: John Mitchel.

Below right: Row of Georgian Houses, John Mitchel Place, Newry.

In 1840, after being admitted a solicitor, Mitchel entered into partnership with Samuel Livingstone Fraser, a successful attorney, and ran the branch office at Banbridge, often defending Catholics against local Orangemen. In 1842, Mitchel became acquainted with Thomas Davis, the friend who, in Mitchel's own words, 'first filled his soul with the passion of a great ambition and a lofty purpose'. The following year, Mitchel and Martin joined Daniel O'Connell's Repeal Association, but only after the death of Davis in September 1845 did Mitchel totally commit himself to politics, and accept a place on the staff of *The Nation*. Sir Charles Gavan Duffy, the paper's proprietor and editor, described him as follows:

> He was rather above the middle size, well made, and with a face which was thoughtful and comely, though pensive blue eyes and masses of soft brown hair, a stray ringlet of which he had the habit of twining round his finger while he spoke, gave it, perhaps, too feminine a cast ...

As early as 22 November 1845 his *Nation* article 'Threats of coercion' caused great controversy, as Mitchel suggested that railways could be sabotaged in an Irish uprising. In June 1846, Duffy was prosecuted for publishing it, but the jury could not reach a verdict. Under the influence of James Fintan Lalor, Mitchel's political views became more radical, and he began to proclaim that peasants should withhold rent to survive the famine.

On 13 May, Mitchel was arrested under the new Treason Felony Act, which he claimed was passed because of him. He was tried at the commission court in Green Street, Dublin, before Baron Lefroy and Justice Moore, on 25 and 26 May 1848, and was sentenced on the following day to fourteen years' transportation. In April 1850, Mitchel arrived in Van Diemen's Land, where he was allowed to reside with John Martin in one of the police districts on a ticket-of-leave. In June 1851, he was joined by his wife and family, and two years later he escaped from Van Diemen's Land with the aid of Patrick James Smyth and his wife, making his way after many adventures to San Francisco.

In later life, he became editor of the *Daily News*, a staunch southern paper. In consequence of his articles which supported the southern cause during the Civil War, Mitchel was arrested by the military authorities on 14 June 1865, and was confined in Fortress Monroe for nearly five months. Later he mused:

> I suppose that I am the only person who has ever been a prisoner-of-state to the British and the American Government one after the other ... I despise the civilization of the

nineteenth century, and its two highest expressions and grandest hopes, most especially – so the said century sees nothing that can be done with me, except to tie me up.

In summer 1874, Mitchel returned to Ireland after twenty-six years of exile. On 16 February 1875, he was elected unopposed for Tipperary while he was on his way once again to Ireland, arriving the following day. On 18 February, Mitchel was disqualified for being a convict, but was again returned by a majority of 2,368 votes on 11 March, when he declared that he would not take his seat. Mitchel died at Dromalane House, Newry, on 20 March 1875. He was buried on the 23 March 1875 of the same month in the Unitarian cemetery, Old Meeting-House Green, High Street, Newry, to the rear of the **Convent of the Poor Clares** which was founded in 1830.

At the corner of John Mitchel Place and William Street is **St Mary's parish church** which was begun in 1810, but wasn't completed until 1819. It was supposed to replace St Patrick's, but the loyalty of part of the congregation to the older place of worship led to a schism within the Church of Ireland community in Newry. This was not healed until 1866, when St Patrick's was completely rebuilt. The memorial tables within the church record the lives and work of many of Newry's prominent citizens. There is a tribute to Dr Davis, the medical superintendent of the workhouse who survived the cholera during the Famine and to Major-General Henry Davis of the 22nd Light Dragoons, who succeeded the Duke of Wellington in the command of Mysore army in India.

From the church, make your way down Kilmorey Street to the area of Boat Street, Quay Street and Custom House Avenue, names which recall Newry's long history as an important port. **The Albert Basin**, completed in 1850, could accommodate ships over 500 tons enabling the textile industry to flourish. **Dromalane Mill**, complete with chimney, can be seen behind the Quays Shopping Centre. This was built in 1816 by William Hill Irvine. His involvement with the linen industry ended in failure but he emigrated to Australia and became Prime Minister of the state of Victoria.

Going along Bridge Street and turning right into Dominic Street is the **Dominican church** which was completed in 1871. The construction of one of the side alters was carried out by the father of Pádraig and William Pearse, who were executed for their part in the Easter Rising of 1916. Turning right into Francis Street you will come to Newry Canal and the Buttercrane. Further along is **Merchants Quay**, stretching from **Buttercrane Quay** to Sugar Island, where you can see some surviving nineteenth-century warehouses. To your right as you leave Cornmarket is McMahon's warehouse with the date 1845 still visible on the wall. During the famine, agents like McMahon provided passage from Warrenpoint for thousands of emigrants to New York, Canada and England.

At the end of the Mall is the **Town Hall** which was designed by William Batt and constructed in 1893. It was one of the last works of the old Newry Town Commissioners, whose crest, dated 1891, can still be seen on the bridge in front of the Town Hall. The style of the building is broadly classical. The most unusual feature of the building is that it is built on a three-arched bridge astride the Clanrye River. The reason was, reputedly, to settle the rivalry between the people of Armagh and Down over which county it should be sited (the river divides both counties).

Moving along Tevor Hill, turn left at the corner of New Street and Canal Quay where one of Newry's most imposing buildings can be seen. **Clanrye Mill** was built on the site if the older mill, which was destroyed by fire in 1872. Designed by William Watson, it has been described as an essay in brickwork. Its style is Venetian and complements the **Riverside Presbyterian church** nearby, which was built in 1866 and designed by William Barre. The style, termed Lombardo-Venetia, is particularly suitable for this site as it was originally surrounded by the river and canal. This red-brick building, with its cut-out stone window tracery, bands and cornices, has circular windows in the east and west gables. The tower is ninety foot high with a pyramidical roof of the diamond-shaped slates.

The Corry Monument in nearby Sandy's Street is a pedimented die and obelisk, mounted on six granite steps. It was erected in 1877, in memory of Trevor Corry who was a magistrate in the town for thiry-five years. The form of the monument reflects the interest in ancient Egypt so fashionable in the mid-nineteenth century. Another member of the Corry family, Isaac, then Chancellor of Ireland, signed the Act of Union in the belief that Catholic Emancipation would follow quickly. It did not, and he became so unpopular that a new road was built from his home at Derrymore House enabling him to avoid the wrath of Newry's citizens. It is still called the Chancellor's Road.

Newry Court House, built in 1843, was designed by Newry architect Thomas Duff, a man who has been described as 'the most important figure in the early development of the architectural profession in Ulster'. This building of stucco and granite construction, topped with a handsome domed copula is generally recognised as his finest classical work and noted by one architectural historian as a building of 'compact elegance'. The building was refurbished in 1994.

Newry is an excellent base to explore the surrounding country. Staying within County Down, the drive along the Carlingford Lough coastline is one of the most picturesque in the country. This large and generally shallow sea lough, forms part of the international border between Northern Ireland to the north and the Republic of Ireland to the south. The lough has an exceptional range of intertidal and sub-tidal habitats found on rock and a range of soft muddy sediments. With such a range of habitats, it is not surprising that the lough supports a diverse range of wildlife; sandwich terns, oystercatchers, redshanks and common seals are all found on the lough.

Four miles from Newry, along the A2 towards Warrenpoint, **Narrow Water Castle** stands on a rock, jutting into the estuary. It was originally built in 1216 by Hugh de Lacy to prevent attacks on Newry via the river. The original was destroyed in the 1641 Rebellion before being rebuilt by the Duke of Ormond in 1663.

Warrenpoint (commonly transcribed into Irish as *An Phointe*, The Point) lies on the northern shore of Carlingford Lough. Lewis, in his *Topographical Dictionary* of 1837, paints an interesting picture of the town and its attractions to the early Victorians:

Narrow Water Castle today.

Far left: Narrow Water, *c.* 1840.

Left: Clonallon church Warrenpoint.

Below: Warrenpoint Port.

The site of the present town was originally a rabbit warren, whence it has received its name. In 1780 it consisted only of two houses, with a few huts for the occasional residence of the fishermen during the oyster season: it now comprises several respectable streets diverging from a square on the sea side, and containing 462 houses, many of them large and well built. This rapid increase has been principally owing to the extraordinary beauty of its situation, commanding very fine views of the bay of Carlingford, and to its convenience as a bathing-town, for which purpose it has been for several years a fashionable place of resort for visitors from all parts.

A railway connection opened on 9 May 1849, increasing Warrenpoint's popularity as a holiday destination. Thousands flocked to the resort every year, where most took the passenger ferry to Omeath in County Lough. Sadly, Warrenpoint railway station closed in January 1965. The ferry remains in operation but only in the summer months, from May to September.

A few miles further along the coast is **Rostrevor**, a beautiful little town on the shores of Carlingford Lough, at the base of the Mournes. The settlement also sits on the Kilbroney River, and at the head of the romantically named Fairy Glen. The name 'Rostrevor' first appeared *c.*1618 and was named after Rose Ussher (the daughter of Henry Ussher, the Anglican Archbishop of Armagh) by her husband Edward Trevor. According to the *Scenery and Antiquities of Ireland* published in 1842:

View over Carlingford from Warrenpoint.

This popular and lovely watering-place is situated on an acclivity, ascending gracefully from the margin of a land-locked bay, and backed by precipitous and lofty mountains; villas, noble mansions, rustic cottages, and every variety of rural dwelling, decorate the lovely scene – a happy combination of mountain and lowland, of wood and water. The rank of the inhabitants contributes to the neat and comfortable appearance of the place; and the public decorations are in character with the greatness and sublimity of the surrounding landscape. A handsome church and steeple are well placed at the upper extremity of the market-place, strongly relieved on the dark front of the mountain behind.

In the town stands a handsome monument to **General Ross of Bladensburg**. Ross fought in Spain under Wellington in 1812, at the battles of Vittoria, Roncesvalles, and the Sauroren. After the conclusion of the war with Napoleon, Ross sailed to North America as a Major-General to take charge of all British troops off the east coast of the United States. Ross personally led the British troops in the attack on the Americans at the Battle of Bladensburg on 24 August 1814, where the American army quickly collapsed. Moving on from Bladensburg, Ross captured Washington D.C. with little resistance. Ross insisted on only destroying public property when he ordered the burning of Washington, including the destruction of the Capitol and the White House.

Ross then organised an attack on Baltimore, Maryland. His troops landed at North Point, twelve miles from the city. During the march, the troops encountered American skirmishers and Ross rode forward to personally direct his troops. An American sniper shot him through the right arm into the chest. Ross died within minutes. After his death, his body was stored in a barrel of 129 gallons of good Jamaican rum and shipped on the British ship *Royal Oak* to Halifax, Nova Scotia, where his body was buried on 29 September 1814.

Above left: General Ross statue Rostrevor, *c.* 1842.

Above right: Rostrevor Pier *c.* 1842.

Rostrevor Main Street.

Rostrevor Town.

Left: Rostrevor, 1920s.

Below: Rostrevor.

Cloughmore Stone

Hanging over Rostrevor is **Cloughmore**, the Big Stone, which was thrown across the mountains by Finn MacCool, the same that tore a piece out of the earth and threw it into the Irish Sea and made the Isle of Man. In fact, this impressive granite boulder was probably transported from Scotland and deposited by retreating ice during the last Ice Age.

Select Bibliography

Bassett, G.H., *The Book of County Down* (Dublin, 1888).

Bryans, R., *Ulster: A Journey through the Six Counties* (Faber & Faber: London, 1964).

Coote, Sir C., *Statistical Survey of the County of Down* (1804, reprinted 1984).

Hanna, D., *The Face of Ulster* (Batsford: London, 1952).

Harris, W., *The Ancient and Present State of the County of Down* (First pub. 1744; Ballynahinch: Davidson, 1977).

Hayward, R., *In Praise of Ulster* (Belfast, 1938).

Lewis, S., *Topographical Dictionary of Ireland* (London, 1837).

McCavery, T., *Newtown: A History of Newtownards* (White Row Press: Belfast, 1994).

Mallory, J.P., *Navan Fort, The Ancient Capital of Ulster* (Belfast nd).

Maxwell, I., *Researching Down Ancestors* (Ulster Historical Foundation: Belfast, 2004).

McCorry, Francis X., *Journeys in County Armagh and Adjoining Districts* (Lurgan, 2000).

Ordnance Survey Memoirs: Parishes of County Down (Belfast, 1990).

Sherman, H., *Ulster* (London, 1949).

Stevenson, J., *Two Centuries of Life in Down 1600-1800* (White Row Press: Belfast, 1990).